DATE DUE

Ledley has truly captured the unspoken challenges of new motherhood. This engaging book is filled with real-life examples, useful information, and helpful strategies that provide support, comfort, and direction. *Becoming a Calm Mom* is a must-read for every woman embarking on the journey of being a mother.

—**Randi E. McCabe, PhD,** *Associate Professor, Psychiatry and Behavioural Neurosciences, McMaster University, and author of* 10 Simple Solutions to Panic *and* Cognitive Behavioral Therapy in Groups

For most women, the first year of motherhood brings intense feelings—from excitement and bliss to loneliness and stress. Faced with dramatic changes in your identity, relationships, mood, and career, it's easy to become overwhelmed and doubt yourself. Fortunately, you don't need to face it alone: Read *Becoming a Calm Mom* for empathic, research-based support to help you confidently navigate and enjoy the journey of new parenthood.

—**Larina Kase, PsyD,** *author of* The Confident Leader *and* The New York Times *bestseller* The Confident Speaker

In this outstanding resource for any new mother, Ledley describes the "hidden" emotional challenges of new motherhood with honesty, warmth, and wisdom. Practical, effective coping strategies for dealing with changes in one's body, identity, and relationships to partner, family, and the world of work are beautifully interwoven with the accounts of other new moms, making this volume a lovely balance of compassion, support, and expertise.

—**Bonnie Ohye, PhD,** *Assistant Clinical Professor, Harvard Medical School, Department of Psychiatry, Massachusetts General Hospital*

Becoming a Calm Mom

Becoming a Calm Mom

How to Manage Stress and Enjoy the First Year of Motherhood

Deborah Roth Ledley, PhD

American Psychological Association
Washington, DC

Published by
APA LifeTools
750 First Street, NE
Washington, DC 20002
www.apa.org

To order
APA Order Department
P.O. Box 92984
Washington, DC 20090-2984
Tel: (800) 374-2721;
Direct: (202) 336-5510
Fax: (202) 336-5502;
TDD/TTY: (202) 336-6123
Online: www.apa.org/books/
E-mail: order@apa.org

In the U.K., Europe, Africa, and the Middle East, copies may be ordered from
American Psychological Association
3 Henrietta Street
Covent Garden, London
WC2E 8LU England

Typeset in Sabon by Circle Graphics, Columbia, MD

Printer: Victor Graphics Inc., Baltimore, MD
Cover Designer: Naylor Design, Washington, DC
Technical/Production Editor: Dan Brachtesende
Cover art: Illustration by Virginia Johnson.

The opinions and statements published are the responsibility of the authors, and such opinions and statements do not necessarily represent the policies of the American Psychological Association.

Library of Congress Cataloging-in-Publication Data
Ledley, Deborah Roth.
  Becoming a calm mom : how to manage and enjoy the first year of motherhood / Deborah Roth Ledley.
    p. cm.
  Includes bibliographical references and index.
  ISBN-13: 978-1-4338-0404-5
  ISBN-10: 1-4338-0404-2
  1. Motherhood—Psychological aspects. 2. Mother and infant. I. Title.

HQ759.L39 2009
155.6'463—dc22
                              2008020164

British Library Cataloguing-in-Publication Data
A CIP record is available from the British Library.

Printed in the United States of America
First Edition

CONTENTS

ACKNOWLEDGMENTS

There are so many people I would like to thank for their unique and important contributions to *Becoming a Calm Mom*.

To Gary Ledley, my husband, my best friend, and my extraordinary partner in parenting: There is so much to thank you for—suggesting the idea for this book, listening to a million scattered ideas and helping me to organize them, and making it possible for me to have the time and freedom to work on this project that has meant so much to me. Most of all, thank you for teaching me such a vast amount about how to be a calmer, more fun-loving mom.

To Jenna and Matthew: Jenna, our first little Ledley, you taught me how to be a mom. Through all the ups and downs of new parenthood, my experiences with you really made me think about how to do this job well. Now, as an almost 3-year-old, you bring me daily joy, giggles, and tons of ideas for a follow-up book on being a calm mom during the "terrific" twos! And, to our newest little Ledley, Matthew, who kept me company during the entire writing of this book (in utero!): I hope you are now reaping the benefits of all that I learned from writing it.

To three super moms—my grandmother, Esther Bernick; my mom, Roslyn Roth; and my mother-in-law, Terry Ledley: I have learned so much from all of you about being a mom and striking that fine balance between family and career. Thank you for your incredible support and love!

To the Bryn Mawr girls: We met at a breast-feeding support group when our babies were only a few weeks old, and I still count on you for friendship, support, and lots of fun. Extra special thanks to Julie Falcone, Jung Lee, Kate Miller, and Sheila Norton.

To my oldest, dearest friends: Melissa Cavelti, Lisa Collins (sister extraordinaire), Tracy Elliot, Lisa Frank, Stephanie Gerstenblith, Kelly Crouch Mazzola, Randi McCabe, Karen Rowa, Christine Samuelian, and especially Andrea Kushnick Rubin: I am so glad we all became first-time moms at roughly the same time in life. It's been amazing sharing this experience with friends I've known forever.

Thanks also to all the women who responded to the Calm Moms Survey.

To Larina Kase: Thank you for encouraging me to write my first "nonacademic" book and for dreaming up the "Calm Mom" name. And to Virginia Johnson for creating the wonderful Calm Mom illustration for my book cover.

And last, but certainly not least, to the wonderful people at the American Psychological Association: Thanks especially to my editor Maureen Adams, who gave me the chance to write this book and helped me every step of the way! Thanks also to the anonymous reviewer who provided so much useful feedback on each and every chapter.

Becoming
^aCalm
Mom

INTRODUCTION

When I was pregnant with my first baby, I had two conversations that I will never forget. Both were with friends who, like me, have PhDs in psychology. Both women are highly accomplished, organized, and competent. They have wonderful husbands and supportive families and friends. They are women anyone would perceive as having it all together. Yet, the two women told me that their first year of motherhood was the hardest year of their lives. Both confided in me about how difficult breast-feeding was and how pressured they felt to continue it despite significant challenges. Both spoke of the loneliness of being home with a baby after spending years in work environments in which they were able to nurture great friendships along with great careers. With tears in their eyes, both mentioned the shame they felt on the days they just didn't enjoy being a new mom. These thoughts and feelings were terribly surprising to my two friends, both of whom had wanted babies for as long as they could remember. When I first had these conversations, I have to admit that they went in one ear and out the other. However, during my daughter's first year, I thought about these discussions again and again. Let me explain why.

When you ask a woman how she is enjoying being a new mom, most talk about the sheer bliss they are experiencing. New moms describe having a baby as "the best thing I've ever done" or "the most wonderful time in my life." When I became a mom for the first time, I was surprised that I rarely (particularly in the first few months) experienced the blissful happiness that so many new moms describe. Rather, each day was a complex blend of emotions. I certainly had many moments of happiness and bliss, but I also had moments of frustration, loneliness, and sadness.

One of the most salient examples of this mix of emotions happened when my daughter was 2 months old. She was very cranky and cried on and off for an entire day. Nothing I did soothed her. Often a walk or an outing to the grocery store gave us both a new perspective. But on this particular day, a torrential rainstorm prevented us from going out. To top it off, my husband was working late that evening, so I had no relief or company to look forward to at the end of the day. I was definitely not having a blissfully happy day! As the day came to a close, I made myself some dinner and put my daughter in her swing next to me at the table. Suddenly, she looked over and presented me with her very first smile. Given the enthusiastic response she got from me, she tried it again . . . and again . . . and proceeded to smile for an entire hour. I abandoned my dinner and started snapping pictures for my husband. It was truly one of those precious new mom moments.

After I put my little one to bed, I called almost everyone I knew to tell them about her fantastic first smile. Yet, I made an interesting observation that night. I was ashamed to share with anyone that I had spent most of the day feeling frustrated and practically crying right along with her when nothing would soothe her. Why was this? When my friends told me about their challenges as new moms, why did they relate their stories to me in hushed tones? Who are all these women who talk about the pure bliss of being a new mom? Were they having a different experience than I was having or that my friends had? Or was there something else going on?

Over the past 2 years, I talked about these issues with every new mom I know. I have concluded that new moms feel a great deal of pressure to share only the blissful moments with others (and trust me, there are many!). They are ashamed to share the challenging moments. They do not want to be perceived as bad, uncaring, incompetent, or selfish mothers. Perhaps more importantly, they do not want to perceive themselves in this way. In particular, women who wanted babies for as long as they can remember or who had a lot of challenges getting or staying pregnant mention feeling that every moment must be special, enjoyable, and meaningful.

The problem with this social pressure to share only the joyful times is that new mothers have no support for dealing with the challenging times. Keeping frustrations and challenges to ourselves can lead to significant anxiety and sadness. It can cause us to focus on the hard parts of being a new mom, so that we fail to recognize and appreciate the many precious and happy moments. Furthermore, by not being honest with friends and family members, new moms fail to benefit from the collective experience of others. The best way to learn how to deal with the challenges of being a new mother is to talk with other people—specifically, to talk with them in an honest and open way.

GAINING INSIGHT INTO WHAT PSYCHOLOGY CAN OFFER TO NEW MOMS

Before becoming a mom, I had spent most of my days talking with other people. I completed my PhD in psychology in 1999 and since then, have focused my attention on the nature and treatment of stress and anxiety. I have done a lot of research and teaching, but my passion has always been my work with clients. It is truly rewarding to help a person who is incapacitated by stress and anxiety move toward a more functional and enjoyable life.

People often joke about how doctors are the worst patients, and I was certainly an example of this during my first few months of motherhood! To be honest, I felt stressed out much of the time. It wasn't until I started to make friends with other new moms that I realized I had all sorts of skills that I could use to adjust to my role as mother. The turning point for me came after I met a group of 10 women and their babies at a breast-feeding support group at our local hospital. We quickly became friends and are still close. For some reason, the typical rules of self-disclosure did not apply within this group of women. We shared everything—the good, the bad, and the ugly about being new moms. When I began to hear other people's experiences (which were similar to my own), I developed clear ideas about strategies that could help them. I had worked with anxious clients for years, so I recognized that my friends and I were experiencing anxiety that is typically associated with major life events (even the exciting, wonderful ones). Although I never practice therapy with my friends, I certainly had little suggestions from my psychologist's toolbox that I offered them. One day I suddenly realized that I had wasted the past few months feeling anxious, but doing absolutely nothing to help myself.

Quickly, I put my "psychologist hat" back on my head and got down to business. I challenged my negative thoughts about my abilities as a mom. If my daughter had a particularly cranky day, I stopped feeling I was at fault. I took a careful look at my standards—for example, what I expected to accomplish in a day—and questioned whether these expectations were reasonable. When I concluded that they were not, I began to set more reasonable goals, thereby setting myself up for success each day, rather than for failure.

I began to be my own behavior therapist, figuring out which factors helped me have great days as a new mom and making sure those factors were included in as many of my days as possible. These factors included being around other people, getting fresh air and exercise, and staying busy. For me, staying busy at home did not do the trick. We spent a lot of time running pretty dull errands, but for whatever reason, on the days my daughter and I got out and about, we both seemed much happier.

I also began practicing the relaxation techniques I had been teaching my clients for years. I used these when my daughter cried inconsolably, when we were being glared at on airplanes because she was not silent for the entire flight, or when I was beyond exhausted but couldn't get back to sleep after a late night feeding.

Perhaps most importantly, I reminded myself of the need to accept all emotions—positive or negative. People want to ignore negative emotion, and they prefer to focus on positive emotion. However, this tendency can lead to the shame, anxiety, and secretiveness that I discussed earlier. I realized that in the safety of our mothers group we talked about everything and that after sharing a particular challenge, I would often feel so much better. One reason for this was that we saw that we were all facing the same challenges. Another reason was that we learned so much from each other through this process of sharing—from solutions to simple problems (which brand of baby bottle or diapers to use) to those that were much weightier (decisions about childcare, the effect of a baby on one's marriage, relationships with parents and in-laws, etc.).

After I started to use the simple strategies that I had been teaching to my clients for years, and after I became more accepting of both the ups and the downs of motherhood, I undoubtedly became a calmer and happier mom. A few months after my first baby arrived, the idea for *Becoming a Calm Mom* was born!

AN OVERVIEW OF *BECOMING A CALM MOM*

I decided to write *Becoming a Calm Mom* after I recognized that I had a lot of advantages as a new mom that others might not have. As a psychologist, I have at my disposal a toolbox of simple and effective strategies to help me navigate challenges in my life. As I mentioned, it took me a while to make the connection between my personal and professional life; however, I saw firsthand the degree to which these strategies could alter my thoughts, feelings, and behaviors on a daily basis. I wanted to share these simple strategies with others. In chapter 1, I discuss what being a new mother is really like (in other words, why new moms are NOT calm!); six Calm Mom strategies are introduced in chapters 2 and 3. The remainder of the book offers countless examples of how to use these strategies in your daily life.

After the six Calm Mom strategies are introduced, *Becoming a Calm Mom* continues with three main sections. Chapter 4, "Calm Mom, Calm Baby," helps new moms deal with the challenges inherent in caring for a newborn. I discuss such topics as feeding, sleep, development, and illness. There are great books available on these topics, so I provide brief tips on how to actually feed your baby or get him or her to sleep, for example. Rather, the focus of *Becoming a Calm Mom* is on you! How can you make decisions about breast- versus bottle-feeding? How can you stop worrying about whether your child is developing normally? What should you do if your fears of germs and illness are preventing you from leaving the house with your new little one? As a new mom, I got a great deal out of reading books on how to breast-feed, but couldn't find much information on the feelings associated with breast-feeding. Similarly, our pediatrician taught us how to clear our daughter's stuffy nose over the course of the 10 colds she had during her first winter in daycare. But no book talked about the guilt I felt about the fact that she was catching all these germs at daycare. *Becoming a Calm Mom* aims to fill this gap.

After the fog of the first few months of motherhood lifts and our babies are eating well, sleeping for longer stretches of time, and starting to do all sorts of exciting things, there is time (albeit not much!) to think about ourselves again. This is the focus of chapters 5 and 6—

moms. In chapter 5, "Remaining Calm When 'Me' Becomes 'Mom'," I discuss solutions to common challenges faced by new moms: the experience of surprising emotions, loss of identity and freedom, loss of self-confidence, and loss of time for oneself. Chapter 6 focuses on the unique challenges facing both working moms and stay-at-home moms. As with the rest of the book, chapters 5 and 6 seek to normalize experiences and offer simple strategies women can use to adjust to their exciting but daunting new role as "Mom."

Chapter 7 is titled "Remembering Relationships: There's More to Life Than Just Your Baby." Our relationships change after we have a baby. Some relationships become much stronger and more meaningful; others deteriorate due to strain. Regardless, all relationships need nurturing, just like our babies. This chapter shows how to use the Calm Mom strategies to effectively deal with spouses, new friends, old friends, and the other significant people in our lives, such as our parents and in-laws.

The final chapter, "Happy First Birthday!," provides a means to reflect on what it means to "make it" through the first year of motherhood. Moms often forget to give themselves credit for a job well done; that is what chapter 8 is all about. Other important topics in this chapter include setting goals for the year ahead and making decisions about whether and when to have baby number two.

Becoming a Calm Mom also includes an appendix and a "Resources for New Moms" section. The appendix addresses the crucial issue of postpartum depression and anxiety. A major goal of this book is to assure new mothers that their experiences and emotions are shared by others; however, some moms will read this book and have difficulty applying the strategies on their own. They might find that their feelings of sadness and anxiety are so intense that they need more assistance than a book can provide. This too is normal—many, many new moms suffer from postpartum depression and anxiety— but there is no reason to suffer alone. There are highly effective treatments available for these problems, including medication and therapy. In the appendix, the symptoms of postpartum depression and anxiety will be reviewed and treatment options presented.

"Resources for New Moms" presents various resources for new moms, from places to connect with other new mothers to great books to read about babies and parenting and reputable Web sites to consult with all your new mom questions.

BECOMING A CALM MOM IS A PROCESS

When I first proposed this book idea the working title was *The Calm Mom*. APA Books suggested I change the title to *Becoming a Calm Mom*. This was an excellent suggestion because learning to be a calm mom is a process. Putting calmness aside, becoming a mom is a learning process. There is an expectation that once your little bundle of joy is placed in your arms in the delivery room, you will immediately know how to be a mom. This is an unrealistic expectation. Learning to care for a baby takes time, as you get to know your baby and your baby gets to know you and becomes familiar with the world. As for being a calm mom, this too takes time. The strategies included in this book are simple to try, but take practice to hone. Read about the strategies, try them all, and then figure out which work best for you. I hope you will come to see *Becoming a Calm Mom* as an honest, open, and fun book to guide and support you through all the amazing "firsts" that will occur during your year as a brand new mom!

CHAPTER I

WHY NEW MOMS ARE NOT CALM MOMS

The moment a child is born, the mother is also born. She never existed before. The woman existed, but the mother, never. A mother is something absolutely new.

—Rajneesh (1931–1990)

You wanted a child all of your life. You waited for years to find the right person with whom to spend your life. Then, it took a little while to actually get pregnant. You spent nine months counting down the days until you would become a mom. You chose names, decorated the nursery, bought clothes, and attended childbirth classes. You felt that your world would be complete after baby arrived. You made it through hours of painful labor, and, finally, your little has one arrived.

Now what?

Becoming a mother for the first time is one of the most miraculous, growth-enhancing, interesting, and fun experiences that life offers.

It is miraculous to finally lay eyes on the individual who has been growing inside you for 9 months. It is amazing to see how beautiful and perfect these little creatures are, from their tiny toes to their soft, downy heads. Although newborn babies don't do much in their first few weeks of life besides eating, sleeping, and filling diapers, it is remarkable to observe how quickly they develop. In their first few weeks of life, babies can imitate others who are sticking out their tongues (try it, you'll see!). By about 2 months of age, babies begin making eye contact and smiling. Soon, babies are working hard to roll over, then to sit up on their own, and before you know it, they are crawling, walking, and talking. It is truly incredible to compare a 1-year-old baby with a newborn. There is probably no other year in our entire lives when we change and grow so much. Although it is certainly fun to watch any baby develop into a toddler, there is nothing like watching your own! Along with the wonder, fun, and excitement is a remarkable feeling of love, responsibility, and pride that we feel for our own children.

It is also incredible to consider all the changes that happen in *your* life between the day you become a mom and the day you celebrate your baby's first birthday. In those first few weeks a woman's hormones go from an all-time high back to prepregnancy levels. As noted in the appendix, this hormonal slide can do all sorts of odd things to new moms, from bringing on torrents of unexpected tears to having strange thoughts that are completely at odds with the unconditional love we expected to feel toward our babies. Two other factors that may contribute to a new mother's wildly fluctuating emotions are sleep deprivation and the body's efforts to recover from the grueling experience of pregnancy and childbirth.

At the same time that our bodies (and minds) are clearly not at their best, there is just so much to learn! New moms must quickly learn how to change diapers, breast- or bottle-feed, bathe, soothe, and entertain our babies. As the weeks and months progress, our brains become flooded with all sorts of new information, from the words of long-forgotten songs and nursery rhymes to the best child care centers or pediatricians in our neighborhoods to the various brands of diapers or bottles we can try.

On a personal level, new moms grow in a myriad of ways. We learn to multitask like never before. Working moms struggle to balance work with home life. Moms who choose to stay home with their little ones have a lot to figure out, too. Some might be transitioning from working outside the home to staying at home for the first time in many years. Those who were not working before having a baby need to figure out how to integrate a baby into an already full and busy life. The first year of motherhood is a time we reshape our identities to maintain what we loved about our pre-baby selves as we incorporate a new identity as "mom." Being a new mom means working on keeping existing relationships strong while developing new relationships that develop because we are now mothers. The first year of motherhood is fascinating not only because we spend it observing the amazing growth of our babies but also because we go through a great deal of growth ourselves.

At the same time, becoming a mother for the first time is one of the most challenging, stressful, exhausting, and overwhelming experiences in life. Although women often seem compelled to paint a rosy picture to others about how blissful it is to be a new mom, the reality is that it is not easy.

WHY IS IT SO DIFFICULT TO BE A CALM MOM?

> The world is full of women blindsided by the unceasing demands of motherhood, still flabbergasted by how a job can be terrific and torturous.
> —Anna Quindlen (2003, p. 48)

To answer the question of why new moms are not calm, I conducted an informal survey of new moms. My survey was done with what psychologists call a "convenience sample." I wrote an e-mail to friends who were new moms and asked them to pass it along to their friends who were also new mothers. This was not a random sample (i.e., getting birth records for a city and calling every tenth person) and certainly not representative of every new mother across America. However, with that said, I think the findings are pretty interesting. I received e-mails from moms all across the United States and Canada, and some from England. Some moms had babies who were just a few weeks old and some had just made it through the first year. Some moms were staying at home with their babies, some working full time, and some working part time. Most had partners who were sharing child care responsibilities; some were on their own. The women in my sample ranged from their late 20s to early 40s. The common thread was that all were writing about their experiences with their first babies—and all had a great deal to say!

The first question in my Calm Moms Survey referred to what respondents found to be the greatest sources of stress during their first year of motherhood. Here are the most common responses I received:

- Sleep deprivation:

  "One of my biggest sources of stress was sheer exhaustion. I remember one night (I think the third or fourth night) when my husband had to literally lift me up so that I could breast-feed our baby."

  "I was not a good napper, so I couldn't nap when my son napped. I was totally running on empty. When he was napping, I tried to get everything done in the house that I would have normally tried to do . . . whether it was realistic or not."

  "I pulled the occasional all-nighter in college to study for a test or get a paper done. I remember feeling sick and totally out of it the next day. I never could have imagined what it would feel like to pull all-nighters for, well, what turned out to be eight months in a row!"

- Loneliness:

  "I went from having company at work all day, everyday, to having minimal company at home."

  "My husband works a lot in the evenings and on the weekends. I thought that when I had a baby, I would never be lonely again. So, it was surprising to actually feel lonelier than I used to, even though I had my baby with me all the time."

- Breast-feeding:

  "I had this dreamy notion that this was the most natural, instinctive thing a new mother could do and that I would have no problem nourishing my child."

  "My loneliness was exacerbated by having trouble breast-feeding, which made me less interested in going out as I felt stressed enough trying to make her breast-feed at home, never mind in front of others."

  "In hindsight I think one of the reasons I had trouble breast-feeding was because of all the pressure I put on myself to be as good a mother as my mom, which only added to my feelings of inadequacy."

- Feelings of frustration, uncertainty, and inadequacy:

  "I had no idea what to do. I always considered myself so smart and now I felt useless."

  "I think the reason it is so insane with our first is because we have nothing to go on. I was so unsure of every move I made. And I felt completely alone. Yes, my husband was there, but I was the mother. I was supposed to know why he [my son] was crying, what would make him happy, and how to get him to stop. The expectations of being 'the one with all of the answers because I am after all, his mother,' was so overwhelming."

  "The most difficult thing for me was not having anything to which I could compare this time of my life. This meant that I had no way of knowing how much better it was going to get and when."

  "Being home with a new baby was hardest for me because I didn't know what to do with myself. There was no order or structure and I was too tired and out of it to make plans. I felt lazy, even though it's one of the most important things I've ever done. I remember vividly standing in the shower and wishing I was going to work because I was 'good at that'."

- Crying:

  "My son cried inconsolably for long stretches for the first few months and I felt completely ineffective most of the time, or at least it seemed there was no rhyme or reason to when I was effective—one day something would work, but by the next day this was no longer what he needed."

  "My baby's constant crying was very hard on our marriage. My husband and I have a good relationship, but we did nothing but fight. It's hard to listen to a baby cry, but when it happens for hours and hours every day, it really wears you down and that's when the squabbling would begin—over ridiculous issues."

  "I have a close group of friends and we all had babies around the same time. All of their babies had very placid personalities, and then there was mine! I hated going in public with her because I felt like a terrible mother. I know it was not my fault that she had these issues, but I felt like people really judged me, even my friends."

- Overwhelming sense of responsibility:

  "When I got married, I felt a new sense of responsibility. Suddenly I had to think of someone else when I made decisions. But this was so much more the case when I had a baby. Suddenly, even the most mundane decisions were important because they affected my baby. It was somewhat overwhelming to realize that this would be the case for many years to come."

  "At the time we had our baby, I was considering moving jobs for the first time in many years. What would have been a difficult decision became an anguishing one. I felt so scared to take any risks with something that involved our family's livelihood because suddenly, there was another person who was completely dependent on me. I had never felt this overwhelming sense of responsibility before."

- Loss of independence:
  "I wanted a baby all my life. I finally had one and now I felt like I want my old life back. I wanted a life of leisure with my husband, my career, a good night's sleep, and gee, I wanted to shower on a regular basis too!"

  "Sometimes my husband asks me what my plans are for the end of the day. This question totally irritates me since my plans are the same at the end of *every* day. I leave work at exactly the same time every day in order to pick up our baby from day care. I can never choose to work later, spontaneously decide to have dinner with a friend, or come home and go to the gym. Everything is planned down to the minute now, and if I do want to deviate and do something for myself, that takes even more planning."

- Imbalance of change in mom's life versus dad's life:
  "My husband's life went on 'somewhat' as usual (taking runs, going to the gym, occasional guys' nights out), while I sat home without a shower, sleep deprived and trying to breast-feed all night."

  "I always felt like I was 'on call.' Even when my husband was around, I felt like no one could do for our baby what I had to do for her."

- Imbalance in career sacrifices for mom versus dad:
  "Whether you stay home, work part time, or full time, it's never quite the same again for a woman. It's the mom who feels the addition of a baby most in her career and how she must juggle it."

- Worry about being a good mom:
  "I had the most amazing mom. It is hard to imagine living up to her."

  "I had a lot of problems with my mom growing up. She remarried when I was young and really had her own life. I worry that I didn't grow up with a model of a good mother. How am I supposed to be one, if I didn't have one?"

- Irrational fears about the baby:
"I would say the factor that contributed most to my stress was fear of something horrible happening to my baby (especially the first couple weeks). It was really hard to shake some of the horrible images I had in my head . . . like falling down the stairs with the baby, dropping the baby, etc. My fear was so great that I unreasonably thought we should move into a different house without stairs."

"When I was driving anywhere with my baby, I would have to turn around and check his seat multiple times to make sure I hadn't forgotten him somewhere."

- Unsolicited advice:
"People seemed to have advice everywhere I went. It was one thing to get it from my mother or friends, but when some woman in line at the supermarket started telling me how important it was to breast-feed when she saw the cans of formula in my cart, I would get really annoyed."

"I didn't mind advice. It just confused me. One person would tell us one thing and another person would tell us a contradictory thing. It took me a few months of being a mom to start trusting my own judgment."

- Change in feelings about one's body and sexuality:
"I didn't feel sexy anymore once I had my baby."

"I didn't realize how long it would take to feel comfortable with sex again. Even when I began to feel comfortable, I was too exhausted to have sex anyway."

"My friends seemed to lose their baby weight so quickly. But, not me. It was terrible to have people ask me when I was expecting when I had a five-month-old baby at home."

THE TROUBLE WITH IGNORING OUR NEGATIVE THOUGHTS

> When we encounter painful content within ourselves, we want to do what we always do: fix it up and sort it out so that we can get rid of it.
>
> —Steven Hayes, PhD (2005, p. 7)

What were your thoughts when reading the responses to this survey? When I asked a few friends to read them, many remarked along the lines of, "Wow, I had those experiences too. I never knew anyone else felt that way." Why did my friends have this sense of surprise when they read the other moms' comments? As Steven Hayes, developer of a novel form of therapy called *Acceptance and Commitment Therapy* explained in the previous quotation, people are not comfortable with *painful content*. They don't want to acknowledge to themselves that they have negative thoughts, and they most certainly don't want to share these thoughts with others. So, they go to great pains to push them away.

Why do new moms feel compelled to keep challenges to themselves? It is an interesting phenomenon because we live in a culture in which it is acceptable to share our thoughts and feelings, even when they are negative, with others. You might work in an environment in which coworkers spend lunch hours griping about the demanding boss, excessive workload, and unjust pay. You might complain to your partner over dinner about your girlfriend who is terrible at returning phone calls, and your partner might complain to you about the terrible calls by the referees during the football game he recently watched. You might get into a heated critique of local or national politics. This type of negativity is a part of daily life and typically goes unnoticed by others.

The rules seem to change when women become mothers. Women seem to feel uncomfortable voicing anything negative about their new roles and responsibilities. New moms do not want to admit that caring for a baby can be challenging. They don't want to say that some days are just not fun. They don't want to admit that they miss going to work or doing things they used to enjoy before having kids. This is the reason a new mom, when asked how she is doing, says, "Great! I've never been happier. Having a baby is the best thing I've ever done."

Where does this secretiveness and shame come from? There are two probable sources. First, women do not want to be judged negatively by others. They don't want people to perceive them as unloving, selfish, or undeserving of being a mom. Second, women do not want to admit to themselves that motherhood is an enormous challenge. Some women assume that skills related to child rearing come naturally and berate themselves if a particular skill or feeling takes time to acquire. New moms also may experience a great deal of guilt if they do not feel blissfully happy every day, particularly if having a baby was a challenge. Many women now rely on technologies to get pregnant, deal with multiple miscarriages before having a successful pregnancy, or must rely on a surrogate or adoption in order to become a mother. All this effort makes women feel that they must appreciate having a baby when it finally arrives. It makes them feel as though they don't *deserve* to voice a negative comment.

There is certainly nothing wrong with being positive. I feel as though I could talk for days about all the wonderful moments I have experienced as a new mom. I will never forget the excitement I experienced when my baby first smiled, sat up on her own, crawled like a wobbly puppy across a whole room, walked across the kitchen, and pieced together a few words to make a real, meaningful sentence. For me, these were all truly miraculous moments.

Why do we need to talk about the negative stuff at all? Simply put, because it is there. All new moms experience downs along with all the ups. And when we suppress thoughts that we perceive to be unacceptable, we end up feeling worse. We feel alone, ashamed, and inept. Furthermore, by keeping things to ourselves, we can never benefit from the experiences of others. By sharing a thought or feeling, even one that seems too terrible to admit, we often learn that others have had the exact same experience. This process, called *normalizing* an experience, can be immensely helpful. Furthermore, when we share with others a problem we are having, they often share a solution they came up with to that very same problem. Rather than struggling alone, new moms can leave a conversation feeling supported and armed with new solutions to very common problems.

THE GOAL OF THE BOOK

> Though motherhood is the most important of all the professions—requiring more knowledge than any other department in human affairs—there was no attention given to preparation for this office.
> —Elizabeth Cady Stanton (1898/2002, p. 112), U.S. abolitionist and campaigner for women's suffrage

Becoming a Calm Mom seeks to accomplish two goals. First, by providing examples of challenges faced by real new moms, the stress associated with being a new mom is normalized. Second, *Becoming a Calm Mom* offers new moms strategies—easy, effective ways to handle the inevitable stress that we all experience during our first year of motherhood. When Elizabeth Cady Stanton wrote the quotation included here, there were no books available on how to change diapers, breast-feed, or help a baby learn to sleep through the night. We are lucky that there are now many books that discuss the basics of baby care. Unfortunately, there is still not much out there on being a mother. I hope that *Becoming a Calm Mom* fills this gap.

LOOKING AHEAD

The six Calm Mom strategies are introduced in the next two chapters of *Becoming a Calm Mom*. By the end of these two chapters I hope you see that there are simple ways to effectively navigate this exciting, but daunting, time in your life. Using these strategies should bring a greater sense of calm to your life and will allow you to more fully enjoy all the miracles and fun that motherhood has to offer.

CHAPTER 2

THREE SIMPLE STRATEGIES FOR YOUR CALM MOM TOOLBOX

The Calm Mom Toolbox includes six Calm Mom strategies. Each strategy can help you through a myriad of situations. Getting advice from our friends, moms, and sisters is great. But the six strategies differ from advice in a few ways. First, the strategies have been used for years in clinical practice, and they truly do lead to improved functioning and a greater sense of life satisfaction. Second, they each involve learning a skill. Rather than having a friend tell you what to do, or tell you what worked for her, these strategies involve a basic process through which you can figure out what works best for *you*. Finally, these skills can be used in many situations. They are helpful not only in your adjustment to being a new mom but are also skills you can use for the rest of your life when stress and anxiety threaten to get in the way of your living a fulfilling and enjoyable life.

In chapter 2, the first three Calm Mom strategies are introduced. Chapter 3 includes the final three strategies. Read through all the strategies and give them a try. See which work best for you.

STRATEGY #1: BE A CALM THINKER

It is remarkable how a woman can go from feeling confident and self-assured one day to being a quivering bag of nerves the next. Yet, this can happen when a woman has a baby. As was clear in the survey discussed in chapter 1, becoming a mom involves acquiring an entirely new set of skills and making adjustments in virtually all areas of our lives. These changes can lead a new mom to view herself very differently than she had just a few weeks before.

One perfect example of this shift has always stood out in my mind. A family friend had a baby when I was in high school. She was a highly accomplished lawyer who had waited until her career was well established to have a child. The baby arrived, and our friend had terrible difficulty breast-feeding. She persevered for weeks and even consulted a nationally recognized expert on breast-feeding. For a reason that now escapes me, this woman simply could not nurse her baby. She plunged into a terrible depression. When my mom came back from visiting this friend when her baby was just a few weeks old, she told me that her friend was barely recognizable. This extremely self-confident woman had spent the entire visit berating herself for being a failure as a mother. Her disappointment in herself over not being able to breast-feed spread to all other areas of baby care. She told my mom that she was incapable of soothing the baby, expressed concern that the baby was unhappy, and lamented that the baby was not sufficiently stimulated in her care and "deserved" to have a nanny.

This is a somewhat extreme example. Yet most women experience some negative thoughts about their abilities as moms. For several decades in the field of psychology, researchers have studied how negative thoughts about ourselves, the world around us, and our futures contribute to problems with depression and anxiety. This understanding led to the development of novel therapies that involve helping clients *talk back* to these negative thoughts. Learning to dispute negative thoughts, rather than accepting them as fact, plays a major role in improving the way a person views her- or himself and the world. Furthermore, when a person sees herself and the world in a more rational way, she tends to function better. Negative thoughts no longer hold the person back from attaining what he or she truly wants in life.

New moms can easily learn to be *Calm Thinkers* by talking back to their negative thoughts, rather than accepting the negative thoughts as fact. As will be the case with the introduction of each Calm Mom Technique, let's consider an example to illustrate this simple and helpful technique:

Example

Jane was spending her first day at home alone with her 2-week-old infant. It was her husband's first day back at work since the baby was born. The past 2 weeks had been fantastic. Jane and her husband had spent hours just gazing at the baby, amazed that he was theirs! While she was busy nursing the baby, her husband did the cooking and cleaning. While the baby slept, they also caught a quick nap or wrote some thank-you notes together or read the newspapers. By the 2-week mark, they felt they had a pretty good handle on this parenting thing.

Everything changed on this particular Monday. Jane was up at 8 a.m. nursing when her husband left for work. Her plan was to shower, get dressed, head out to do grocery shopping and errands, come home, clean the house, and prepare her husband his favorite dinner. It took until 9 a.m. to finish feeding the baby. Jane put him in his bouncy seat on the bathroom floor and turned on the shower. The baby began to cry. Jane checked his diaper and indeed, he needed a change. After he was clean and dry she tried to put him down, but the crying began again. She gave up on the shower for the time being and rocked the baby until he fell asleep. At 10 a.m., she finally got him back into his bouncy seat and got herself in the shower. Jane took a quick shower, got dressed, dried her hair, and was ready to head out. When she picked up the baby to put him in his car seat, he woke up and spit up all over her, himself, and the floor. Jane needed to change her clothes, change the baby, and clean the carpet. It was now 11 a.m., and the baby began to fuss. It had been 3 hours since he last ate, and he was ravenously hungry.

Jane sat down to feed her little one. Negative thoughts began to come—quickly and furiously. "I am such a loser. I can't believe it's almost noon and I haven't left the house yet. I'm sure every other new mom is out of the house at this point in the day." "My husband is going to be furious if he comes home to a disastrous house and no dinner." Jane's eyes welled up with tears. When the baby was finished eating at noon, Jane put him down for a nap and promptly fell asleep herself. When he woke her up at 2 p.m., her thoughts about herself were even harsher. Worse, it was time to feed the baby again. By 3 p.m., Jane felt too overwhelmed and drained to pack up the baby and the diaper bag to head out. She turned on the television and put the baby down next to her to do some tummy time. When her husband got home at 6, she was feeding him again. She felt bad that she had not even made it to the grocery store, let alone cooked a delicious dinner. As her husband whisked the baby away for a bit of daddy time, Jane burst into tears, thinking, "I am a failure, I can't do this," and "I must be the only woman on earth who can't manage being a wife and a mother."

There is no doubt that Jane's thinking was problematic on this first day of being home alone with her baby. Her negative thoughts left her feeling sad and angry at herself. Her thoughts made her doubt her abilities—not only about what she was able to do today, but what she would be able to do in the future (i.e., balancing being a mom and a wife). Her thoughts even affected her behavior. While she had a window of opportunity to leave the house at 3 p.m., she had become so down on herself that she simply turned on the TV and gave up her plans for the day. While it is perfectly reasonable (and important) for new moms to put their feet up and relax for a while every day, in this case Jane let her choice reinforce her belief that she was a failure.

Becoming a Calm Thinker is a simple process. It just involves some thought! The first step is to **become aware of your thoughts.** Sometimes negative and disparaging thoughts come so quickly and furiously that we barely notice that they are there. Yet, they have a major effect on how we feel and behave. It is possible that Jane was not even aware of what she was thinking on her first day at home alone with the baby. However, she was aware of feeling sad and angry. She knew she was tearful and she knew that she avoided leaving the house when the opportunity to do so presented itself. The key to becoming a Calm Thinker is to become aware of the thoughts that are driving feelings and behaviors. The way to do this is to ask yourself, "what am I thinking right now?" Picture your thoughts as butterflies flitting around in your head. As a Calm Thinker, you want to grab your butterfly net and capture these thoughts. When you are first learning to be a Calm Thinker it can be helpful to write down the thoughts as you capture them.

The next thing to do is **question your thoughts.** Are your thoughts reasonable? Would you say what you are saying to yourself to other people in your life, such as your sister or best friend? Is there a different way to think about the situation? After you pose these questions to yourself, it is essential that you **answer the questions.** Answering them helps you come up with a calmer way of thinking.

There are a few ways to engage in this process of questioning your thoughts. If you have already noted your negative thoughts, pose these questions and then write your answers. If you have not written down your thoughts, ask yourself these questions in your head and respond to them. Talk out loud if you need to! Remember, a baby loves to hear mommy's voice. Particularly at the time you are just learning how to think calmly, you can ask a trusted loved one or friend to help you with the process. For example, Jane could share her thoughts with her husband and ask him to help her question them.

The final step in becoming a Calm Thinker is to **come up with a calming statement.** This statement summarizes what you learned after capturing your negative thoughts, questioning the thoughts, and generating answers to your questions. This calming statement should bring you into a rational, helpful way of thinking. It can also be used the next time you experience similar thoughts. When you become aware of a negative thought, you can short cut to the calming statement that you generated the last time you had the same negative thought.

How did this work for Jane? When Jane's husband came home from work, he played with the baby for a while, put him to bed, and called to order a pizza. He then sat down with Jane to ask her about her day. Tearfully, she reported what happened and shared her negative thoughts about herself. Jane's husband was shocked at her reaction. First, he questioned whether it was reasonable for her to go shopping and cook a fancy meal on her first day home alone with the baby. Second, he pointed out that she had accomplished an immense amount during the day. She had fed the baby four times since he left for work (with each feeding lasting for one hour). She had changed countless diapers. She had kept the baby clean, cuddled with him, and gave him some tummy time. She had taken a shower, gotten dressed, and even took a nap. He was impressed. He pointed out that most women in the same situation would have had a pretty similar day. As he had three sisters who have young kids, he realized that having a newborn in the house was no piece of cake. He reminded Jane that she had never criticized his sisters for having had a similarly "unproductive" day when they had their babies.

Essentially, Jane's husband became her surrogate Calm Thinker for the day. As she heard him argue with her thoughts, she realized that his points were valid. When the next day went pretty much the same as her first day at home with the baby, she reminded herself, "keeping a new baby fed and clean and loved is a great accomplishment for a day." This calming statement helped her through the first few weeks of motherhood until the baby's needs allowed her more flexibility to fit other activities into her day.

One important point to note about Calm Thinking is that many of the derogatory thoughts that new moms have about themselves are faulty in some way. New mothers are hard on themselves. They set such high standards that they are setting themselves up for failure. They say things to themselves that they wouldn't say (or even think) about their best friends or sisters. These thoughts should always be questioned and reframed with the Calm Thinking strategies.

However, not all negative thoughts need to be fixed. New moms are terrified to admit to having any negative thoughts. The first few months at home with a newborn can be boring from time to time. As soon as a new mom has the thought, "I'm a bit bored," or "I wonder what's happening at the office right now?" she may immediately shift to such derogatory thoughts as, "I'm a terrible mother for thinking this way." Being at home with a new baby can also be incredibly frustrating, particularly on fussy days when nothing will calm the baby down. New mothers might think, "This is so hard," "I'm so frustrated," or "I just wish the baby would stop crying." These thoughts immediately progress to "I bet other moms don't get frustrated like I do," or "I shouldn't be complaining about this because I am so lucky to have a baby."

It is essential that new moms realize that thoughts are just thoughts. They are just collections of words. As humans, we have labeled certain words *positive* (e.g., happy) and certain words *negative* (e.g., frustrated). By nature, we relish positive thoughts and are ashamed of negative thoughts. Negative thoughts make us feel bad and affect our behavior in similarly negative ways (Jane choosing to not leave the house, even when an opportunity for doing so presented itself). We try to suppress or ignore negative thoughts by telling ourselves not to think these thoughts at all. As anyone who has been on a diet can attest, trying not to think about food makes us think about—guess what—food. It is the same with negative thoughts. The more we try to ignore them, the more intense and frequent the thought becomes.

With this in mind, the other essential part of being a Calm Thinker is to **become accepting of all thoughts**—negative or positive. If you have the thought, "I am frustrated," or "I am bored," try accepting it. Don't get carried away with what the thought means. Being bored or frustrated does not equal being a terrible or undeserving mother. Rather, these are just states of being that can quickly change when your baby does something exciting for the first time, when an old friend calls to see how you are, or when you go out for a walk and see that your favorite tree has started to bloom. Despite what some people tell you, the day-to-day life of a new mom is not uniformly exciting, rewarding, and fun. Rather, it is a hodgepodge of thoughts and feelings. The precious moments are undoubtedly all the more precious when they are mingled with other moments that are challenging or mundane.

Take a look at the list of steps under Becoming a Calm Thinker.

STRATEGY #2: BE YOUR OWN BEHAVIOR THERAPIST

Many psychologists spend a great deal of time with clients identifying and changing problematic behaviors. Clients come to us with specific problems, usually involving doing too much of something (such as overeating) or not doing something they would like to be doing (such as exercising). We spend time figuring out why the problematic behavior is persisting, even when the client would like to change it. Then, we implement behavior change plans to help clients become and stay

---

Becoming a Calm Thinker

1. Become aware of your thoughts. ("What am I thinking *right now?*")
2. Question your thoughts. ("Does this thought make sense? Would I say this to my sister or my best friend? Is there a different way to think about the situation?")
3. Answer the questions posed in the previous step.
4. Come up with a **Calming Statement** that summarizes what you have learned after capturing your negative thoughts, questioning the thoughts, and generating answers to your questions.

Remember: **be accepting of *all* thoughts—both positive and negative.** Negative thoughts ("I feel frustrated right now . . .") are only problematic if they spiral downward into disparaging thoughts about yourself (". . . so, I must be a terrible mother"). Allow yourself to experience negative thoughts, just as you allow yourself to experience positive thoughts.

---

healthier and functional. For example, I learn that a client only over-eats while watching television alone in the evenings. To change this behavior I suggest that the client try doing something with her hands (such as knitting) while watching TV at night so she cannot eat, or that she watch TV with her roommate, in whose presence she typically does not overeat. Similarly, I learn that a client who avoids exercising is ashamed to work out in front of other people because he is overweight and out of shape. With this client I suggest starting an exercise program by walking in his quiet neighborhood instead of going to a busy gym, or meeting with a personal trainer in his home. The idea is to figure out why people get stuck in a rut of problematic behavior and to then draw up a plan in which they can make subtle changes so that they feel better.

The great thing about these *behavior modification techniques* is that they are easy to use and effective. You do not have to have an advanced degree in psychology to be your own *behavior therapist!*

Let's see how these strategies apply to new moms by presenting examples from two families, each dealing with a common challenge that can arise when there is a new baby in the house.

Example One

Steven is an 11-month-old baby who still does not sleep through the night. At bedtime, his mom rocks him to sleep. They sit together in a rocking chair until Mom is absolutely certain that Steven is deeply asleep; at this point, she puts him in his crib. During the night, Steven's parents have found that the only way to get him back to sleep when he wakes up is to go through the whole rocking routine again. They are now doing this one to three times per night. Because it takes about 30 minutes for Steven to fall back asleep, Mom and Dad are getting very little sleep themselves.

Example Two

When Doug and Annette brought little Patrick home from the hospital, Doug wanted to be involved in all aspects of his care. The minute he came home from work he wanted to change Patrick's diaper, give him a bath, or play with him. Annette, the parent who provided the majority of the baby's day-to-day care, had developed specific ways of doing things with Patrick. When Doug took the initiative to care for Patrick, Annette would hover over him and correct everything he did, wanting to show him "her" way. The result of this was by the time Patrick was 4 months old, Doug had basically checked out on his parenting responsibilities. Now when Doug came home from work he would sit down and turn on the TV or grab the newspaper. Annette constantly complained that Doug didn't help with the baby.

Behavior therapists are really good at figuring out what maintains problematic behaviors, and new moms can learn to do this too.

The trick is to identify a **trigger,** a **response,** and a **result.** Let's consider this for baby Steven and then for Doug and Annette.

The **trigger** for Steven is his need to fall asleep. His **response** to being sleepy is to cry; his parents' **response** is to rock him. The **result** is that Steven can only fall asleep by being rocked.

The **trigger** for Doug and Annette is Doug helping with the baby. Annette's **response** is to criticize and correct. The **result** is that Doug stops helping with the baby, and Annette is unhappy that she has to do everything herself.

Clearly, the results of both these situations are problematic.

The next step in being your own behavior therapist is to figure out what **goal** you want to achieve. Steven's parents want him to sleep through the night. Doug wants to be involved with the baby and Annette, on her own terms, wants the same thing. The only way to accomplish these goals is to break the cycle of trigger and response. The way to do this is to **change the response.**

When it is time to go to bed (trigger), Steven's parents rock him (response). And, when he wakes during the night and cries because he can't get back to sleep, his parents rush in and rock him back to sleep (response). The problem is that Steven has never learned to put himself to sleep. Therefore, when he wakes up at night, which all people do, he doesn't know how to get back to sleep on his own. The only way out of this for Steven's parents is to stop rocking him; instead, they should put him in his crib when he is awake so that he learns to go to sleep on his own (goal). If he can fall asleep on his own, he will also learn to do this in the wee hours when he wakes up.

In the case of Doug and Annette, Annette criticizes Doug (response) when he is taking care of the baby (trigger). Over time, Doug stops taking care of the baby. Annette has led him to believe that everything he does is wrong. Because Doug wants the baby to get the best care possible, he defers to Annette. Furthermore, he begins to avoid the situation that brings on the criticism in the first place. Doug has been feeling shut out of parenting, and Annette is feeling alone in the responsibilities involved in taking care of a newborn. The problem is that Annette has such high standards that she turned Doug off from helping. Her perfectionist standards have caused her to be in the mess that she is now in. The only way out of this cycle is to invite Doug to be involved, permit him to do things his own way, and praise him for helping, even if he has done things in a less than perfect way. Only then will Doug feel comfortable getting back into parenting and only then will Annette be getting the help that she needs (goal).

There is a simple set of rules for acting as your own behavior therapist. Identify a trigger, response, and result for a problematic behavior. Figure out what goal you would like to accomplish. Then, decide how to change your response so you can realize this goal. This general strategy is discussed throughout this book. It can be applied to a baby's behavior, as in the example of Steven; to day-to-day life as a mom; and to our interactions with other people, as in the example of Doug and Annette. Acting as your own behavior therapist is a humane technique for getting what you want out of others and for getting what you want out of yourself as well.

There is one important caveat. Making behavioral changes can be really difficult. The basic rule of thumb is that things often get harder before they get easier. It is easy to fall into a routine. Even if a routine is not working well, a person will often continue with it because staying with a known behavior is often easier and more comfortable than making changes. Acting as your own behavior therapist is going to take patience as well as faith that things will get better if you stick to the plan.

Let's return to our examples one last time to demonstrate. Steven's parents decided they were ready to start "sleep boot camp" with their 11-month old son. They recognized that the only way out of this sleep issue was to get Steven to fall asleep on his own. They discussed the problem with their pediatrician, consulted books, and decided to go cold turkey. They would put Steven down and let him cry himself to sleep. In the middle of the night, they would come in for a quick check and a little pat on the back. They would then leave and let Steven get himself to sleep again. They were expecting a couple of very trying weeks. The first night, Steven cried for over an hour before first falling asleep; on two other occasions during the night, he cried for about 20 minutes. Steven's parents supported each other and decided they would not go to him, regardless of how bad they felt. They recognized that Steven needed to learn an important life skill—putting himself to sleep. On the second night, the crying time decreased. It continued to decline for 3 more nights. On the fifth night, Steven whimpered for a few minutes when they left his room, but they didn't hear a peep out of him for the rest of the night. It was the first time in his life that he slept through the night. There is no doubt that these 5 nights, especially the first few, were heart wrenching to these loving parents. Yet, it wasn't as bad as they had predicted. Within 5 nights, they had a little boy who could soothe himself to sleep. Mom and dad began to feel more well-rested too.

How about Doug and Annette? Annette initiated a discussion with Doug about wanting him to be more involved with the baby. She conceded that she had been overly critical and promised to take a more hands-off approach. Doug was enthusiastic about having special times alone with his son. On the first day of their new behavioral plan, Doug came home from work and whisked the baby away from his tired mom. He took him upstairs for a bath. When they came down, the baby was dressed in pajamas that Annette felt were too hot for the weather that day. But she didn't say anything. An hour later, Doug and Annette were eating dinner and the baby was doing some tummy time next to the table. Suddenly, a stain began to spread across the back of the baby's pajamas. Annette lost control. She yelled at Doug for not putting the baby's diaper on correctly. She took the baby back upstairs to bathe him again and get him ready for bed. Doug's feelings were terribly hurt. When the baby was asleep, Doug and Annette discussed what had happened. They considered throwing in the towel and returning to the old pattern of Annette doing everything for the baby. Both were unhappy with this idea. They agreed that Doug needed time to learn the skills associated with caring for a baby—as Annette had when the baby was first born—and agreed that he deserved the chance to become comfortable with his own way of doing things. Although it was difficult for Annette, she took a hands-off approach for the next few nights. Soon, Doug was comfortable with taking care of the baby. He even felt confident enough to ask Annette for tips on how she did things. When he finally felt like a team player, he felt it was safe to let his guard down. When Annette began to see that one task could be successfully completed in different ways, she too became more open to learning from Doug and other people in her life.

In both examples, the process of behavior change was not easy. However, the payoff was big. The keys to succeeding are simple—patience and perseverance.

See sequence of steps in the list, Becoming Your Own Behavior Therapist.

STRATEGY #3: BE A CALM COMMUNICATOR

When a baby is born, virtually every relationship that his or her parents have changes. The relationship between the parents changes. The interactions the baby's parents have with their own parents and with their in-laws change. Suddenly, private lives may be discussed at the workplace, as new parents need to negotiate changes in schedules and responsibilities with their bosses. As parents, we enter into relationships we have never had before, such as with child care providers. These new relationships might require a level of assertiveness never needed before, because after all, babies will not be able to speak for

---

Becoming Your Own Behavior Therapist

1. Identify a **Trigger,** a **Response,** and a **Result** (e.g., **Trigger:** Dad helping out with the baby. **Response:** Mom criticizes and corrects. **Result:** Dad stops helping with baby care and mom is unhappy that she is doing everything herself).
2. Figure out what **Goal** you want to achieve (e.g., **Goal** is to have both mom and dad involved in baby care).
3. Figure out how to **Change your Response** so that you can realize your goal (e.g., Allow dad to do things his own way and praise him for helping).

Remember that making behavioral changes is not easy and things can sometimes get worse before they get better. **The keys to success are patience and perseverance.**

---

themselves for many years to come. All these changes in relationships require excellent communication skills. Although it is inevitable that some relationships will feel the strain of a new addition, knowing how to be a *Calm Communicator* will help lessen the strain on the new family.

It is ironic that communication skills are so important at the same time parents are facing the effects of sleep deprivation. Let's be honest: sleep deprivation can make the most even-tempered person irritable. This irritability undoubtedly affects how we communicate with others. Suddenly, even small requests can come out as barking demands. This can take new moms and the people in their lives by complete and utter surprise!

New moms can learn to become better communicators, even when they are sleep deprived. They can also teach these communication skills to important people in their lives. There are three basic styles of communication—two can get us into trouble, but one works like a charm to get us what we want out of life while being respectful of others. Following is an example that illustrates these three styles.

Example

Lindsey had always been close with her mom. They typically spent at least one evening a week together having dinner or seeing a movie. But after Lindsey's baby was born 2 months ago, she began to feel her mother was intrusive. Her mother, who had recently retired, did not have much to do each day and had taken to dropping in on Lindsey and the baby without notice. She would simply use her key to open Lindsey's front door—as early as 8 a.m., or as late as dinnertime. Whenever she arrived, she expected her precious grandson to be awake and ready to play.

Over the past few weeks, Grandma had visited at particularly inopportune moments. One morning Lindsey had been trying to get a bit of extra sleep as the baby slept. And one evening, her husband had brought home a romantic dinner for her. Having mom around was not on the schedule for the night! This particular visit was the final straw, and Lindsey knew she had to say something to her mother.

The first style of communication is called **passive communication.** Passive communicators are concerned about appeasing others but do not look out for their own needs. When passive communicators talk they avoid eye contact, hunch their shoulders, and speak quietly. If Lindsey used the passive communication style with her mom, she would say, "Thanks for coming over, Mom. It's always nice to see you. Come any time!" This kind of statement would be respectful of the needs of Lindsey's mother. However, it would not accurately represent what Lindsey felt, nor would it help her meet her own needs.

The second style of communication is called **aggressive communication.** Aggressive communicators look out for themselves but neglect the needs and feelings of others. When aggressive communicators talk, they tend to glare at people or even look down on them (e.g., standing up when the other person is seated); they tend to speak loudly and with a hostile tone. If Lindsey used this communication style with her mother, she would say, "Get the heck out of here, Mom. If you come over again without calling first, we're going to have a real problem on our hands." Although her mother would likely respond to this kind of statement (i.e., Lindsey's needs would be met), there would undoubtedly be a lot of hurt feelings along the way. Furthermore, although Lindsey might feel relief that she got this off her chest, she would likely feel bad about herself in retrospect.

The third style of communication is **assertive communication.** Assertive communicators strike a delicate balance—their needs are met, but they also take into account the needs and feelings of others. Assertive communicators tend to make eye contact and speak in a firm but warm tone. Assertive communicators are definitely calm communicators. They are not so reserved that they are dominated by others. but they also are not bullies. If Lindsey used the assertive communication style with her mother, she would say, "Mom, I know you love to spend time with the baby. We love it. too. However, it would be best for you to call first and plan a time. That way, the baby and I can be ready to spend some fun time with you."

Basically, Calm Communicators follow four steps:

- They **consider the other person's perspective.**
- They **voice their own perspective.**
- They **tell the other person what they need.**
- They **offer a solution** that might be equally acceptable to both parties.

Mom would probably comply with Lindsey's request for planning her visits because she sees the benefit to her—regular meetings with her grandson when he is awake and ready to play. Lindsey's needs are met, too. She has control over the times her mother visits and is able to ensure that the timing of a visit works as well for her and the baby as it does for her mom.

The three styles of communication are summarized in Becoming a Calm Communicator.

As with other effective techniques, Calm Communicating takes practice. When people are tired and stressed out, they tend to become exaggerated versions of themselves. People who are typically passive become more neglectful of themselves because they don't have the energy to speak up. People who are typically aggressive communicators begin to bully more than usual because they don't have the resources to control their outbursts. To learn to communicate calmly, we have to practice frequently. When we are feeling as though our resources are low, we need to remind ourselves that it is important to

---

Becoming a Calm Communicator

Avoid being a passive or aggressive communicator:

- **Passive communication:** Passive communicators try hard to appease others, but their own needs are not met.
- **Aggressive communication:** Aggressive communicators look out for themselves, but they neglect the needs and feelings of others.

Be a Calm Communicator by using Assertive Communication:

- **Assertive communicators** have their own needs met and look out for the needs and feelings of others.

To Be a Calm Communicator:

- **Consider** the other person's perspective.
- **Voice** your own perspective.
- **Tell** the other person what you need.
- **Offer** a solution that might be equally acceptable to both parties.

---

communicate so our own needs are met while being respectful of the needs of others.

LOOKING AHEAD

In this chapter, the first three Calm Mom strategies were introduced: Calm Thinking, Being Your Own Behavior Therapist, and Calm Communicating. In chapter 3, the remaining three Calm Mom strategies are presented. After you learn all the strategies in the Calm Mom Toolbox, try them out. See which strategies work best for you. And remember that you will become better at all the strategies with practice.

CHAPTER 3

THREE MORE SIMPLE STRATEGIES FOR YOUR CALM MOM TOOLBOX

In chapter 2, the first three Calm Mom strategies were introduced. We learned how to become Calm Thinkers, our own behavior therapists, and Calm Communicators. Chapter 3 includes the final three Calm Mom strategies. Remember to try each one out to see how each works for you.

STRATEGY #4: THE CALM MOM APPROACH TO MAKING DECISIONS

New moms often feel challenged by the need to make decisions. Many new mothers remark that they have difficulty making everyday decisions such as what to wear or what to make for dinner. Although these minor decisions can be stressful, new moms also face the need to make significant decisions during their first year of motherhood, including whether to return to work or what arrangements to make for child care.

Decision making is difficult for new moms for a number of reasons. The significant hormonal changes that occur after delivery contribute to the stress a new mother feels. Even after our hormones settle down, however, ongoing sleep deprivation can maintain decision-making difficulties. During my first few months of motherhood I suddenly changed from being a decisive person to one who literally could not decide which grocery store I wanted to go to. It seemed completely ridiculous that I could spend the entire morning thinking about the pros and cons of my various choices.

The bigger decisions about work, child care, and similar issues are difficult because their impact goes so far beyond ourselves. It is probably the first time in our lives we have to consider so many viewpoints other than our own. What choice is best for the baby? What choice works best with the choices my partner is making? What choice can I live with, too? These decisions are so overwhelming because the pros and cons of different options might be very different for the various people involved.

Making Little Decisions

Before presenting the Calm Mom Approach to Making Big Decisions, let's discuss quick tips for making little decisions—those pesky choices about where to shop for groceries or what to wear that can seem so overwhelming in the first sleep-deprived months of motherhood.

The first tip is to **set time limits.** Give yourself 5 minutes to decide what to wear, what errands to do, or which household chores to tackle each day. After you make your decision, don't agonize over it or change your mind! This is not to say you shouldn't be flexible when you need to be. If you had planned to head out to buy a baby gift for a friend but realize you are almost out of diapers, it is certainly appropriate to change your plans. But if you choose to wear a black shirt and then start wondering whether you should wear a white shirt, keep that black shirt on and get going with your day!

The second tip is to **make your choices automatic.** For example, no one likes doing housework, but it is a necessary part of life. It is unrealistic to try to clean your whole apartment or house in a single day when you are taking care of a new baby. It can be helpful to select one chore to accomplish per day. New moms often feel so over-whelmed by selecting this one chore that they end up not doing any at all, and then they feel incompetent and lazy, which of course they are not. A great strategy is to make a weekly schedule, listing one chore each day. This eliminates the pressure to make a decision at a time when doing so feels too overwhelming.

The final tip is to **get busy with something else.** Rather than spending a significant chunk of your day brooding over an insignifi-cant decision, set the time limit discussed previously, mentally turn your decision-making switch to the *off* position, and get busy with something else. One way to do this is to carry through with your deci-sion right away. If you have decided what to wear, get dressed right away and move on with your day. If there is a time delay between making your decision and acting on it (e.g., if you decide which gro-cery store to go to in the morning but aren't planning to go shopping until noon), get busy with something that will occupy your mind. Get down on the floor and play with the baby. Call a friend. Read the newspaper. Do a crossword puzzle. Check your e-mail. Get your mind busy with something more productive and interesting.

Making Big Decisions

Making big decisions involves a slightly more in-depth process. But it is a process that works. When faced with making big decisions, we are often so overwhelmed that we either avoid making them at all or jump to a poorly thought out decision just to resolve the issue. Furthermore, people often fall into the trap of wanting to make the perfect decision or wanting to make a decision that will work for years to come. When we set ourselves up for such impossible goals, avoidance can take over. The Calm Mom Approach to Making Decisions takes an over-whelming task and gives it structure. This approach involves a number of simple steps and a way to go back later and check in on your decision to make sure it is working out as planned. Let's begin with an example, and demonstrate the technique from there.

EXAMPLE. Lori decided to return to work after having her baby. She is comfortable with this decision, as she loves her work and feels confident that she can balance it with a satisfying home life. Her dilemma is what to do about child care. She is so overwhelmed by this decision that she recently asked her boss for another month of maternity leave so she can figure things out. Every time she begins thinking about what to do with her daughter, Sarah, she gets so stressed out that she just drops the topic. She recognizes that there are many options but has trouble sorting out her feelings about the pros and cons of each. It is usually on Mondays, the beginning of the workweek, that Lori realizes that she must make the decision soon, or she will lose her job.

The Calm Mom Approach to Making Decisions involves six steps:

1. Define the **problem** and set a **goal**.
2. **Brainstorm** at least five possible solutions.
3. Consider the **pros and cons** of each solution.
4. **Select** one solution or a combination of solutions.
5. Make a plan to **implement** the solution.
6. After giving the solution a chance, **evaluate** whether or not it is working.

The Calm Mom Approach to Making Decisions includes a worksheet that will help you easily follow these steps.

Let's return to our example to see how the process works. One evening, Lori and her husband sit down to work through their decision-making process.

The Calm Mom Approach to Making Decisions

THE PROBLEM:

_____

THE GOAL:

_____

Possible Solutions (at least five)	Pros	Cons

SOLUTION that I will try first (Can be a combination of solutions):

_____

_____

_____

PLAN for implementing the solution: _____

_____

_____

I will evaluate whether or not my plan is working by _____ (date) and consider other possible solutions if it is not working.

---

1. The **problem** is difficulty making a decision about child care for Sarah. The **goal** is to make a decision. This might seem like an overly simplistic goal—it does not include any values. Why didn't Lori set the goal of making a *perfect* decision, one that

would work now and well into the future? The most important part of setting a goal is that the goal must be measurable by an objective standard. There is no objective way to assess whether a decision was the perfect one. It is easy to measure whether Lori and Jeff accomplished *making a decision* because either Sarah would enter a child care arrangement or she would not.

Another reason why it is important to set objective goals is that we often cannot make value judgments about our decisions until we try them out. Even if Lori and Jeff heard from friends that a certain day care was fabulous, it would be impossible to know what they think of it until after they enrolled their own child and tried it out. The beauty of the Calm Mom Approach to Making Decisions is there is a step at the end of the process that cues you to go back to evaluate your decision after it has been implemented and you have adequate data to go on.

2. Lori and Jeff brainstormed **possible solutions** to their problem. It is great to come up with at least five possible solutions. Sometimes decisions are so overwhelming that people pick the first solution that enters their mind without considering alternatives. Selecting at least five solutions ensures that you give consideration to a range of possibilities. Lori and Jeff came up with the following:

- Use day care.
- Hire a nanny.
- Send Sarah to the lady down the street who looks after two other children in her home.
- Have Lori's and Jeff's moms spend alternate days caring for Sarah.
- Have Lori quit her job and stay home with Sarah.
- Have Jeff quit his job and stay home with Sarah.

In the brainstorming phase, it can be helpful to write down all possibilities, including those you might not have previously considered. Lori had always planned to go back to work, and the couple had never even considered having Lori go back to work while Jeff stayed home with Sarah. However, realizing that these solutions were within the realm of possibility, Lori and Jeff wrote them down and agreed to give them fair consideration.

Next, Lori and Jeff weighed the pros and cons of each of their six options:

- Day care. Pros: licensed by the state, lots of people around to monitor quality of care, good social interaction, lots of learning opportunities. Cons: expensive, kids catch each others' illnesses, stressful to get Sarah out of the house in the morning, someone would have to miss work if Sarah were sick or if day care were closed.
- Nanny. Pros: one-on-one attention, less stress getting out of the house in the morning, less exposure to illness, no concern about sick days or day care being closed. Cons: expensive, no one else around to monitor quality of care, limited social interactions, someone would have to miss work if nanny were sick or went on vacation.
- Lady down the street. Pros: affordable, convenient, great caregiver-to-child ratio, some social interaction, potential for learning opportunities. Cons: no one else around to monitor quality of care, someone would have to miss work if caregiver were sick or went on vacation, some exposure to other kids' illnesses.
- Grandmothers. Pros: total trust, no cost, development of great relationship between grandparents and Sarah. Cons: difficult to ask the grandmothers to do things a certain way, lack of social

interaction with other kids, might be scheduling conflicts because of other commitments.

- Lori or Jeff staying home. Pros: total trust, no cost, Sarah spends most formative years with a parent, parents could ensure social interactions and learning opportunities. Cons: loss of income, stay-at-home parent missing out on fulfillment derived from work.

Lori and Jeff individually considered the pros and cons of each choice and shared their top choice when they each arrived at one. Both selected the in-home day care run by the lady down the street. They liked that Sarah would have some social interaction with other children but would also receive a lot of attention from her caregiver, who only looked after three children at a time. They knew that Mrs. Smith's house was packed with educational toys and that she did not let the children watch television. So, they felt confident that Sarah would spend stimulating days at her house. Although they would have to get her up and ready to go in the morning, the distance to the caregiver's home was so short that they did not expect it to be stressful. When they considered the cons of this option, they recognized that they were not terribly serious. After speaking with other families who sent their children to Mrs. Smith's home, they learned that she rarely got sick and that she was completely trustworthy.

Finally, Lori and Jeff decided that it would be reasonable to evaluate their choice in 3 months. A great advantage of this decision-making process is that Lori and Jeff were left with several other options that could work if the in-home day care did not. They could still pursue commercial day care, hire a nanny, have their moms care for Sarah, or even reconsider having one parent stay home. Realizing that they had good options helped make their decision easier. It did not need to be a permanent choice because if it did not work out, there were many other choices available.

As with the other Calm Mom strategies, effort is involved in the Calm Mom Approach to Making Decisions. It is a process that involves a lot of thought and, therefore, a commitment of time. Ironically, new moms are faced with making these big decisions at a point in their lives when their time is terribly limited. However, there is no doubt that making time for decision making pays off. It prevents us from avoiding making decisions at all, or making snap decisions that have little thought behind them. Ask a family member or babysitter to watch the baby and go to the park or coffee shop to give yourself a chance to really think. After you arrive at a decision, set a specific date to evaluate whether your decision is working or whether you need to revisit the process to come up with a better solution. And finally, remember that very few decisions are set in stone. Making decisions can be so much easier when you remind yourself that you can change your mind. Furthermore, it can be soothing to remind yourself that a decision made now does not have to work forever. Knowing that you have a method you can use to make future decisions as your needs or preferences change can be reassuring.

STRATEGY #5: A CALM BODY AND SOUL

Many factors associated with being a new mom make you feel stressed. Sleep deprivation can most definitely make you feel as though your nerves are on edge. When your baby cries, particularly when she is inconsolable, you can also feel as though you are at the end of your rope. Being out in public with babies can be stressful, because they are unpredictable. We can all relate to people in a restaurant or in line at the supermarket who glare at us because our babies are wailing. Throughout *Becoming a Calm Mom,* I talk about the experiences that jangle the nerves of new moms and how to deal with them. In the meantime, there are three simple exercises you can do to achieve a calmer body and soul during these stressful moments.

I have taught these three exercises to my clients for years. I found myself using them at various times during my first year of motherhood. I used them frequently when my little one was having a cranky day. On some days, I would try every trick in the book to soothe her and nothing worked. At these times, I opted to try to relax myself; often, this had a great effect on her too. I used these exercises when she was fussing in a public place such as an airplane, and I was trying to shift my focus away from the critical faces of people around me (some of whom would also offer horrid advice, such as the woman who handed us a giant, crunchy pretzel for her to chew on when she did not even have teeth!).

I used the exercises a lot on the two or three nights that we initiated what we called *sleep boot camp*. At about 7 months, our pediatrician told us that our daughter no longer needed to be fed at 4:00 a.m.—she just wanted a visit with us. He told us to stop going into her room when she cried at this hour; within a few nights, she would finally be sleeping through the night. He was completely correct, but staying in bed when she was crying for those few nights required some serious relaxation on my part!

Most of my clients end up with a preference for a particular relaxation exercise over the other two. My recommendation is to try all three and see what works best for you.

Breathing Exercises

When we are anxious or stressed out, we tend to unconsciously hold our breath or breathe shallowly. Pick a time you are experiencing a totally calm moment to try this: Hold your breath for as long as you can, or get a very narrow straw (e.g., a coffee stir stick) and breathe through it for a minute or two while holding your nose closed. What do you feel? I have done the coffee stir stick exercise with rooms of college students; many would get into quite a panic after a moment or two. They got dizzy and lightheaded, they worried that they were not getting enough oxygen to their brains, and their hearts started to race and pound. This, in essence, is what we do to ourselves when we are anxious. Shallow breathing starts to make us feel panicky and this in turn makes a stressful moment seem even scarier and more fraught with potential disaster.

When you notice yourself getting stressed out, check on your breathing. Are you holding your breath or breathing shallowly? If so, take a time out and concentrate on breathing deeply. Take a refreshing inhale through your nose, and slowly let the air out through your mouth. Close your eyes while doing this exercise to make it easier to focus on keeping your breathing slow and even. Make sure not to exaggerate the slowness or deepness of the breathing, however. Sometimes breathing too deeply can induce anxiety. Work on your breathing for at least 5 minutes and notice how the slower, more controlled breathing refreshes you.

One advantage of breathing exercises is that you can do them anywhere. You can do them while stuck in a traffic jam with a hungry baby. You can do them in the middle of the night when the baby is having trouble nursing. You can even do them if another person frustrates you and you want to gather your thoughts before replying. Getting used to the breathing exercises might take a bit of practice. Try it a bunch of times and adjust the pacing so it feels comfortable for you.

Muscle Relaxation

In addition to changes in breathing, many people experience changes in muscle tone when they feel stressed. Specifically, people tend to become wound up like springs when they are nervous! The next time you are feeling stressed, check on your body. Are you holding tension anywhere? Many people hold tension in their faces and necks, which can contribute to tension headaches. Others tend to tense up their stomach muscles or even their backsides (which under different conditions can be very good exercise!).

Muscle relaxation involves noticing the difference between tension and relaxation in all muscle groups of your body. Making the shift from tension to relaxation helps people feel less stressed out and more able to face frustration. It is best to practice muscle relaxation in a comfortable place, while lying on your bed or stretching out in a recliner. Begin with your face. Scrunch up your facial muscles as if you have just eaten a very sour lemon. Hold that tension for 30 seconds. Then, with a nice exhale out through your mouth, let go of the tension. Relax all those facial muscles. Feel the tension float away. Notice the difference between tense and relaxed muscles. Then move on. Progress to your shoulders. Scrunch them up until they touch your ears, hold for 30 seconds, and release. From this point, you can tense and relax your arms (do a tight bicep curl), your stomach muscles, your thighs and backside, and your legs and feet (hold your legs straight out and flex your feet). When you have tensed and relaxed all these major muscle groups one by one, tense up your whole body at the same time. Then, do a full release and let your body stay as limp as a rag doll for a couple of minutes.

Muscle relaxation is a little less transportable than breathing exercises. Yes, you have your muscles with you wherever you go—but muscle relaxation is more noticeable to others and can get in the way of other activities, such as driving! When my clients become adept at muscle relaxation, they find that they can shorten it to the final step—tensing and releasing all muscle groups together, rather than doing one at a time. This can be done quickly, in almost any situation (e.g., when trying to get to sleep at night, when the baby is crying loudly at the grocery store, when you are about to embark on a difficult conversation with someone important in your life).

Positive Imagery

Positive imagery involves transporting yourself to a wonderful place in your mind when the real life around you is stressful. Here's how it works. Begin by considering what your favorite place is in the world. Many people select a beautiful beach. Others prefer mountains, forests, or a beautiful vista in their favorite city. The goal is to select a place that you love but also one that is calm, peaceful, and relaxing. After you settle on a place, close your eyes and set aside some time to vividly picture it. Positive imagery works best if you use all your senses. Here's an example of a positive imagery script that uses all five senses:

> You reach the end of your mountain hike. You find a smooth boulder to sit on. You take your heavy pack off your shoulders and gaze at the vista. You see high peaks, some snowcapped. Farther down the peaks, there are forests of lush green pine trees. And, at the very bottom of the mountain, the place at which you started your hike, is the most beautiful azure blue lake. Despite it being hot down there, it is cool and crisp high in the mountains. The air feels wonderful as it gently wafts through your hair and over your hot skin. The air smells even better than it feels. It is so fresh and clean, with a slight hint of pine. There is very little sound up here. You hear some birds and the slight rustle of wind. There are other hikers around but they are respectful of the silence. You get a ripe peach out of your bag and take a bite. It is a perfect peach, sweet, juicy, and delicious. As you eat, you continue to gaze at the view, wondering if there is any more beautiful place on earth.

Positive imagery is a great strategy because it is transportable—it resides in your mind. This is the strategy I have used on airplanes to block out the stares of irritated passengers as my daughter struggled with plugged up ears. I have found it helpful to sit, rock her, and zone out to my beautiful place! You can share the image with the baby by describing it to her. As a baby feels her mom becoming relaxed and hears the sound of a calm voice (rather than a plaintive one imploring, "Please, please, stop crying!"), many babies will relax themselves.

Other Relaxation Strategies

I encourage you to try the three relaxation strategies to see which will work for you. You can also try combining the exercises. For example, you can do deep breathing while picturing your positive image. Or, you can set aside 15–20 minutes per day for relaxation time and do all three exercises in succession.

Mothers can also think about what was relaxing to them before having a baby. Having a new baby is so overwhelming that we often forget to rely on the simple strategies that worked for us for years. Make a list of these relaxing things. Consider things such as listening to music, going for a walk, doing yoga, calling a friend, taking a bath, or making a cup of herbal tea. Keep your list handy—when you are feeling overwhelmed, select an item and give it a try. Chances are that if the strategy worked for you before you became a mom, it will work for you now.

Many moms worry that if they do something to help themselves relax, it means they are neglecting their babies. This couldn't be further from the truth. Obviously, it is important to make sure your baby's needs are met before you focus on yourself. But remember that taking care of yourself often rubs off on your baby. When you turn on a yoga tape and start easing your tension, you might find that the calming music also lulls your little one into a Zen-like state!

For a summary of relaxation exercises see the Tips for Creating a Calm Body and Soul.

Tips for Creating a Calm Body and Soul
Try the following relaxation strategies to create a Calm Body and Soul: • Breathing exercises • Muscle relaxation • Positive imagery • Listen to music • Dance with your baby in a sling or infant carrier • Take a bath or shower • Go for a walk • Do yoga • Call a friend or family member • Do anything else that you used to find relaxing before having a baby

STRATEGY #6: CALM COMPANIONSHIP

The final Calm Mom strategy involves companionship. Becoming a new mom changes our existing relationships and changes our need for relationships in many ways. Relationships are discussed in greater detail in chapter 7. This chapter offers tips on nurturing your existing relationships and growing new ones. Unlike other Calm Mom strategies, seeking *Calm Companionship* does not involve set rules or steps. Rather, it involves an attitude toward relationships.

Make Time for Relationships

Raising a baby is a full-time job. On top of that job, many new parents have paying jobs as well. It often feels as though there isn't time to go to the bathroom, let alone time to nurture relationships. Yet doing so is an absolute must for your health and well-being—and for the health and well-being of your child. Your child will learn about the social world from you, and if you don't make time for others in your life, he won't have a model for having others in his own life.

For many new moms, the most important relationship they must attend to is the relationship they have with the father (or other parent) of their new baby. Many new parents talk about the blow to their relationship after a new baby arrives. There are undoubtedly many factors that contribute to this, but time is definitely an important one. Sometimes it can feel as though days go by and partners barely say hello to one another—and when they do, conversation revolves around the baby. At the end of the day, it is certainly fun to discuss what the baby did all day. But relationships need more than this.

First, parents need to talk about themselves. When one spouse returns to work and the other stays home, both feel uncertain about what to discuss at the end of the day. The working parent often feels guilty about taking attention away from the baby. And the stay-at-home parent often feels as though they will bore their partner to death if they talk about how many times the baby ate that day or how many diapers he or she filled. The bottom line is that sharing experiences brings people closer. The nature of the experiences is not terribly important. What is important is feeling connected and supported in whatever we do.

Second, parents need to schedule couples time. We often feel as though we are terrible parents if we want a night out without the baby, but in fact the opposite is true. Time away is actually great for the baby because it strengthens the relationship of the parents. Many new parents feel as though a few hours alone together is the best way to nurture the marriage and have meaningful conversations. Particularly when an important issue needs to be discussed (e.g., a decision about child care, returning to work, household responsibilities) it can be crucially important to have a few hours of uninterrupted time to really work things out. If it is impossible to get someone to watch the baby or if you feel uncomfortable leaving the baby, schedule time to have these important discussions. This means picking a time when the baby is likely to be napping, and then turning off the TV, phone, and e-mail and completely focusing on each other.

It is also perfectly acceptable to go out without the baby simply because it is fun for you and your partner. Again, many parents feel guilty about doing things for themselves. A great way to reframe this thought is to recognize that time away—time that strengthens relationships—ends up benefiting the baby immensely.

It is also important for new mothers to make time for other relationships in addition to that with one's spouse. Few of us have as much time to see our girlfriends or family members as we did before becoming moms. However, even a couple of hours per month can make a difference. Going to get a manicure with a friend, meeting someone for a game of tennis, or attending a monthly book club can give you a whole new perspective on being a mom. This time away allows you to share experiences, get back in touch with your premotherhood self, and talk about something other than babies!

Be Honest in Your Relationships

Being honest in relationships means sharing both the good and the not so good. By doing so, you will be doing a favor to yourself and others. Difficult thoughts and feelings must be dealt with. If we push them away, we end up thinking about them more. Furthermore, by labeling them as *bad* or *wrong* we end up feeling bad about ourselves. When we talk about the whole range of thoughts and emotions that new moms experience, a few things happen. First, the challenging stuff often doesn't sound as bad after we say it out loud. Second, when we share experiences we often find that other people are having the same experiences as we are. Finally, through sharing we can learn solutions from others that we might not have thought about by ourselves.

When you are honest in a relationship, you also give others the license to be honest. If you tell your partner what you find difficult about being a mom, he will feel more comfortable telling you what he finds hard about being a dad. When you share your real experiences with friends, they know that they can be honest and share with you. This doesn't mean that all your time with others needs to turn into gripe sessions. What it does mean is that when you are bothered by something, you have set up in your relationships an arena in which both parties feel they can seek support and advice.

Look Out for Yourself in Relationships

It is ironic that at a time in our lives when we are most in need of support and advice, we spend most of our time with a little person who cannot utter one word! It is also ironic that at this time of need, our time is so limited. What this all adds up to is the importance of quality over quantity. Perhaps at no other time in our lives is it as important to look out for your own needs in relationships and to surround yourself with people who meet these needs.

It is difficult to define what this means exactly, and you may think that the previous sentence sounds selfish. However, taking care of yourself is a good thing and not selfish at all. Let's be a little more precise by considering some examples.

EXAMPLE ONE. Leslie had a difficult mother-in-law. When she and her mother-in-law, Bea, were alone, Bea gave Leslie a hard time about everything. She criticized her for breast-feeding, constantly remarked on her shoddy housekeeping, and insisted that she not go back to work after the baby turned 3 months old. Bea, who was an adoring mother, was quite different when Leslie's husband was around. Bea would compliment Ben on his recent accomplishments at work, his new haircut, and, of course, his gorgeous baby. Leslie wouldn't mind Bea if she only had to see her when Ben was around. Although she never complimented Leslie about anything, at least she was not critical in the presence of her son.

Leslie began to find that her mother-in-law's visits had a profound effect on her. Mostly, she found herself feeling incredibly annoyed and frustrated. This translated into less patience with Ben and with the baby. To a lesser extent, Leslie also found that she worried more after seeing Bea. For a few days after a visit, Leslie would obsessively question whether she should go back to work even though on many days she was looking forward to doing so.

Finally, she discussed her concerns with Ben. The couple discussed various ways to deal with this problem. Ben decided that his top priority was protecting Leslie while also nurturing a good relationship between his mom and her new grandson. They decided that the best way to accomplish this goal was to have Bea visit only when Ben was home. Although Leslie still was not thrilled with her mother-in-law, she was at least able to protect herself from the assaults on her self-esteem she had regularly been enduring.

EXAMPLE TWO. Jeanne had been friends with Lois since college. Lois had always been a negative person. Despite having a pretty good life, Lois was perpetually unhappy. Jeanne had tolerated this for years, but after she had a child she noticed that her attitude was changing. Her time to go out to do things with friends was extremely limited, and she found that spending time with Lois was a real "downer." Lois had an excellent job, owned a home, and had recently become engaged to a nice guy. However, during their last visit Lois dominated the conversation with complaint after complaint. She griped about an expensive bill from the plumber, an irritating coworker, the incompetence of the seamstress who was altering her wedding dress, and even the weather. At the end of dinner Jeanne realized she had barely spoken a word. She never had a chance to tell Lois about her new baby or to get any support about the new challenges she was facing. Instead, she listened and supported Lois.

Although Jeanne was always prepared to help her friends in times of need, it seemed as though Lois was always in a time of need. When Lois called a few weeks later to make dinner plans again, Jeanne decided to decline. She had no intention of ending her friendship with Lois; rather, she decided that she would prefer to spend her next free evening with a friend who she could listen to and support, but one who would also support her.

As you notice from both examples, the suggestion is not to abandon people simply because they don't serve your needs! Instead, think about how to strengthen your social life. This often entails making slight changes, as in the case of Leslie visiting her mother-in-law only when her husband was with her, or Jeanne deciding to pass up a dinner invitation from Lois. For Leslie, this slight change led to a great improvement in her self-confidence and self-esteem. For Jeanne, it meant spending her next free evening with a friend who was slightly more attentive to her needs.

Don't Neglect Others' Thoughts, Feelings, and Needs

The preceding tip pertains to looking out for yourself in relationships. At the same time, it is essential not to neglect the thoughts, feelings, and needs of the other people in your life. Many new moms recognize that they become focused on themselves during their first year of parenting. The task of raising a child seems so overwhelming and important that it is hard to imagine that anyone else has anything quite so pressing going on in their lives! This can cause new mothers to talk endlessly about their own problems and about everything their precious baby is doing, forgetting that other people have interesting lives too!

Make sure you ask friends and family members how they are doing. Try as best you can to offer them the help and support that they need. Doing so can have a number of positive results. First, by helping others we increase the likelihood that others will want to help us (after all, new moms do need help from time to time!). Second, becoming immersed in someone else's life can be refreshing when all our focus is on our babies. We don't get much positive feedback from babies for all that we do for them. Yet listening to a friend or bringing a sick relative a meal can elicit warm thanks that make new moms feel that they have accomplished something worthwhile.

Seek Out Other People in Your Situation

When we become parents it is essential that we work on maintaining the important relationships we already have in our lives. However, at this time of immense transition we might find that we need to develop new relationships—particularly with women who are also new moms. Meeting other mothers can help you navigate your first year of motherhood in many important ways. Sharing experiences can help us see that other new moms are dealing with the same challenges that we are. Furthermore, by sharing experiences we learn an immense amount from others. Meeting other new moms can also improve our moods. A day at home with a baby can seem endless—and as many new moms mentioned in our survey, quite lonely. Planning to meet up with another new mom for a walk, lunch, or a play date can greatly improve the day. The "Resources for New Moms" section at the end of this book presents a number of suggestions on ways to connect with other new moms in your area.

For a summary of Calm Companionship tips, see the Tips for Calm Companionship.

Tips for Calm Companionship

- **Make time for relationships.** Remind yourself that making time for relationships—and the relationship with your partner, in particular—is *not* selfish. A strong, loving parental relationship is one of the greatest gifts you can give to your baby.
- **Look out for yourself in relationships.** Tailor your relationships so you get what you need (love, support, fun, etc.), while also feeling good about giving back to others.
- **Don't neglect others' thoughts, feelings, and needs.** Don't be baby-centric. Make sure to ask friends and family members what is going on in *their* lives.
- **Seek out other people in your situation.** Meet and connect with other new moms. People in the same boat you are in will likely be a great source of support, advice, and fun.

LOOKING AHEAD

All six strategies in the Calm Mom Toolbox are now at your disposal. Remember to give each strategy a try to determine those that work best for you. Keep in mind that you become better at using each strategy with practice—so keep using them in a variety of situations.

In the next chapter the Calm Mom strategies are put into action. The focus in chapter 4 is on babies. Read on to learn how you can more calmly cope with all the challenges that having a new baby in your life can present.

CHAPTER 4

CALM MOM, CALM BABY

In this chapter, the focus is on babies. During your first few months of motherhood, most of your focus will be on your baby, too. Foremost in your mind will be figuring out ways to soothe, feed, and care for this helpless little creature for whom you are now completely responsible. It's a little daunting! There are many books available on all aspects of baby care. *Becoming a Calm Mom* takes a different perspective—namely, how moms can deal with their anxieties about caring for their little ones. In this chapter, simple tips on the basics of baby care are given, but most of the discussion is devoted to challenges you face as a new mom. Each baby care topic will be divided into three sections: The Facts, The Challenges, and The Solutions. Of course, The Solutions will focus on how to use the six simple Calm Mom strategies that are introduced in chapters 2 and 3.

WHAT ASPECTS OF BABY CARE DO NEW MOMS WORRY ABOUT?

In chapter 1, our Calm Moms Survey was introduced. Here in chapter 4, results from the next survey question are discussed. Our panel of new moms was asked, "What aspect of baby care did you find most difficult in the first few months?" Of the moms who responded, almost half of them mentioned breast-feeding. The next most common response was difficulty with sleep—several new moms mentioned problems with the baby's sleep and some mentioned problems with their own sleep (or lack thereof!). Other responses included difficulty soothing a cranky baby, worry about how to entertain the new baby, and concerns about the baby's health. Although none reported worrying about their baby's development, this issue will also be covered in this chapter. On the basis of personal and professional experience, my sense is that moms often compare their babies to others to ensure their own little one is developing appropriately.

THE THREE BASIC CALM MOM TIPS ON BABY CARE

A few general tips can be helpful, regardless of the exact nature of baby care that is stressing you out. These tips are the following: (a) Take all advice with a grain of salt; (b) be flexible; and (c) be a Calm Communicator. Let's consider each in turn.

Take All Advice With a Grain of Salt

The Calm Moms Survey showed that many new moms feel daunted by their lack of knowledge about how to care for a baby. Many women who give birth have never changed a diaper, bathed or dressed a baby, or been responsible for soothing a little person who has been crying for hours (or what seems like hours!). Even women who had some of these experiences have never nursed a baby until their own child is placed in their arms. This lack of experience can turn a confident woman into one who feels completely clueless! Inexperienced moms seek out information on baby care from various sources— books, relatives, friends, doctors, and Web sites. Whether they like it or not, new mothers also get a lot of unsolicited advice. New moms are barraged by vast amounts of information about baby care. As if the sheer quantity were not bad enough, all this information can be wildly inconsistent.

When large amounts of inconsistent information are combined with a self-doubting mom, you have a real recipe for disaster. New moms feel completely overwhelmed, tend to make snap decisions about baby care, and then beat themselves up if the decision yields an unfavorable outcome.

Consider the example of Juliette, a new mother who was encouraged by her friends to buy a popular baby care book. Juliette felt so uncertain about how to care for a baby that she strictly followed the guidelines in this book. Some rules seemed a little rigid to Juliette, but she stuck to them nonetheless, assuming that the author of such a popular book must know better than she did about caring for a new baby. The book recommended a strict feeding schedule, but Juliette's baby started to cry with hunger an hour before the book said she should. The book recommended letting the baby cry at night so he or she would learn to sleep through the night, but even after several nights of trying this approach, both Juliette and her baby were up much of the night crying! Juliette spent much of her days trying to soothe her distressed baby—and trying to console herself. A few weeks after Juliette began following the book, she really started beating herself up. She thought, "Wow. You can't even figure this 'mom stuff' out with a book telling you what to do. Maybe you aren't cut out for being a mother."

At her lowest point, Juliette met another new mom in the park (she was out for her scheduled fresh air time as dictated by "the book"). This other mom seemed amazingly relaxed and happy. As they began to chat, Juliette started to cry, explaining that she was a complete failure as a new mom. She mentioned that she couldn't succeed despite following this particular baby care book that so many other moms raved about. Juliette's new friend began to laugh and stated, "That book is horrid. I read half of it and literally tossed it in the garbage." She went on to discuss her approach to parenting— which seemed more intuitive, sensible, and relaxed to Juliette. Juliette went home, put her book away, and tried some of the suggestions her new friend had made. Within a few days, she felt enormously better about being a new mom.

There is nothing wrong with seeking advice. New moms can learn an immense amount from parenting books (see the appendix for suggestions that are consistent with the Calm Mom approach), relatives, and friends. However, before acting on advice, use your Calm Thinking strategies. Take a step back and ask yourself: "Does this make sense to me?" "Does this fit with my developing philosophy of parenting?" and "What are the potential advantages and disadvantages of doing things this way?" Even when advice seems sensible, it is essential to take into account your personal values and lifestyle and consider whether the advice is consistent with them. It is fine to listen to advice, consider it, and then say, "Interesting, but not for me." At the same time, other advice will seem completely sensible and will become part of your approach to parenting.

Be Flexible

Making decisions becomes much easier when you take a flexible approach. Juliette's biggest problem was not trying the suggestions she read about in her parenting book. Rather, it was sticking to these suggestions when she intuitively felt that it was not right for her or her child. Juliette equated giving up on the book with failure. Her negative thoughts clouded her sensible side and prevented her from being flexible.

Although we might not want to admit it, caring for a baby involves trial and error. Does the baby sleep better when swaddled or when his limbs are free? Does he drink better from Brand A bottle or Brand B bottle? When he is fussy, does he calm down best in mommy's arms, a bouncy seat, or a swing? New babies are constantly learning about their worlds, and we are constantly learning about them. It takes flexibility to learn what works best in various situations.

Decisions are also easier to make when we know that they do not need to be permanent. This is particularly true with decisions made prior to baby's arrival. Many parents-to-be make firm decisions about feeding, pacifier use, sleep arrangements, and so on. It is great to think about these issues before the baby comes and to discuss these issues with one's partner. Yet in reality, it is impossible to know exactly how things will turn out until you actually have a baby. Again, parents should not feel like they have failed if they go back on a decision they made before having all the available information. I was firmly opposed to pacifiers before having a baby (at this point, I can't remember why!). On the second day our daughter was home from the hospital, she was crying inconsolably; we decided to try giving her a pacifier that came as a free sample with baby bottles we had purchased. The minute we popped it in her mouth, she started sucking happily and within a few minutes was fast asleep. Within days, our whole view on pacifiers had changed. They worked as a soothing strategy for our daughter until she matured a bit and was able to soothe herself. A bit of flexibility and openness to trying things in new ways can make baby care easier.

Be a Calm Communicator

Most issues of baby care are not resolved by the new mom alone. Rather, moms make decisions about baby care with their partners. New moms must also discuss baby care choices with child care providers to ensure consistency for the baby throughout the day. Furthermore, new moms often find themselves defending decisions about baby care to people in their lives who dole out advice, solicited or not. Opportunities abound for practicing Calm Communication skills!

It is difficult to communicate calmly about matters related to baby care. First, these matters are often discussed when you are at your least calm and rational. If you are sitting on a bench in the mall trying to nurse your crying child, you might not have a great deal of patience for a woman who sits down next to you and starts extolling the virtues of formula. If you are working on getting your baby to sleep through the night, you might not have much patience with your spouse at 3:00 a.m. if he wants to go in to soothe the baby.

Second, matters of baby care are fraught with emotion. People have strong opinions on breast versus formula feeding, establishing healthy sleep habits, and appropriate child care. There will be countless times during the first year of motherhood when you find yourself at odds with a person with whom you are talking.

Whenever possible, try to have important discussions about baby care at low-stress times. Discussing theories on sleep in the middle of the night when the baby is ferociously crying is not going to get you anywhere. Talk about it at a time of relative peace and quiet, when a sleep battle is not going on. Whenever possible, try to formulate a plan before the stressful situation occurs. If you are working on getting your baby to sleep through the night by letting him soothe himself back to sleep, agree with your spouse in advance how often you will go in to check on him and how you might be able to help each other deal with the stress of an upset baby.

Also, always be mindful of the main goal of assertive communication: taking into account the other person's needs while looking out for your own needs. If you feel strongly about a certain decision, be sure to acknowledge the other person's feelings. At 3:00 a.m. you can say, "Honey, I know you would really like to bring Joe into bed with us right now. I would like to let him get back to sleep in his own bed. Remember, over the weekend we decided that what we both want is for Joe to learn to sleep through the night on his own. Let's leave him alone tonight and talk about it again tomorrow when our minds are clearer." This message comes across much better than, "If you go and get that baby, I am going to be furious with you." Even the most passive person can become quite aggressive in the middle of the night!

With these three general tips established, we now focus on specific aspects of baby care.

FEEDING

The Facts

In the Calm Moms Survey, over half the respondents cited breast-feeding as the biggest challenge they experienced in caring for their babies. Let's consider some statistics before we discuss the challenges associated with feeding babies. The American Academy of Pediatrics (AAP; 2004) recommended that a newborn be breast-fed without supplemental foods or liquids for the first 6 months (known as "exclusive breast-feeding"). Despite this strong recommendation, few American women meet this goal. The most recent data available on breast-feeding in America comes from the 2002 National Immunization Survey conducted by the Centers for Disease Control. Li, Darling, Maurice, Barker, and Grummer-Strawn report on the 2002 data in their 2005 paper in *Pediatrics*. These data are fascinating. The survey differentiates between "any breast-feeding" and "exclusive breast-feeding." About 70% of women try breast-feeding at least once. By the time their infants are 7 days old, 59% are breast-feeding exclusively and 68% are breast-feeding with supplemental formula. By 1 month, these numbers drop to 52% and 62%, respectively. By 6 months, only 14% of moms are exclusively breast-feeding and only 36% of moms are breast-feeding with supplemental formula.

Why do so few women breast-feed (and even fewer breast-feed exclusively), despite the recommendations from the AAP? These data suggest that breast-feeding might not come as naturally as we are led to believe! Let's consider the challenges associated with feeding babies.

The Challenges

I interviewed Terry Sanborn, a registered nurse and lactation consultant at Bryn Mawr Hospital in suburban Philadelphia, about why women stop exclusively breast-feeding (personal communication, July 16, 2007). Consistent with what is written in many books about breast-feeding, Ms. Sanborn cited four main reasons women stop breast-feeding their babies: (a) worry about having enough milk for the baby, (b) pain, (c) lack of family support, and (d) a return to work. She suggested that worry about having enough milk and breast pain contribute to early discontinuation of breast-feeding (in the first few weeks).

The mothers who responded to the Calm Moms Survey spoke eloquently about the challenges Ms. Sanborn cited.

- Worries about insufficient milk supply. "Because I had a low milk supply I had to pump after every feeding and give her some more milk. This meant I was spending my whole day either breast-feeding, pumping, or giving bottles."
- Pain. "One of the reasons breast-feeding was so hard for me in the first 6 weeks was physical discomfort. I am an obstetrician, but even so, I was surprised by this."
- Family Issues. "When I was struggling with breast-feeding, I got conflicting advice from two women I really respect. My mother-in-law had exclusively breast-fed her children and loved the experience. She encouraged me to continue. My mom did not breast-feed and she encouraged me to stop. It was hard to know which way to go."

- Return to Work. "Although I was physically comfortable with breast-feeding by the time I went back to work, I definitely started cutting back at this point. I hated lugging the pump to work. It was also a huge challenge to find a time to pump. I shared an office, so I needed to kick out my office mate (who thankfully was also a new mom), plan around meetings, and put a big sign on the door requesting no interruptions. I was constantly nervous that someone would barge in. Some days, my pumping would get delayed and I would worry about leaking all over my shirt. It was no picnic!"
- Other challenges cited by moms included the time commitment of breast-feeding ("As I was exclusively breast-feeding, I was the only one who could feed my baby during the night. This contributed to months of sleep deprivation"; "I felt like breast-feeding was all I was doing.") and discomfort with breast-feeding in public ("I had a hard time getting used to 'exposing myself' in public.").

With so many challenges, it is no surprise that moms often stop nursing soon after they start and why so few moms meet the goals set by the AAP.

In this chapter, I focus on the challenges associated with breast-feeding. This focus came about because so many moms who responded to the Calm Moms Survey discussed the stress they experienced while nursing their little ones. It is interesting that none of the moms who responded to the Calm Moms Survey talked about the challenges of bottle-feeding, but there is no doubt that such challenges exist for many women. Feeding a baby by breast or by bottle is a time consuming job. For moms who bottle-feed, there is the increased time commitment of cleaning and preparing bottles. Bottle-feeding can be tricky because babies don't necessarily take to the first kind of bottle they are given or to the first kind of formula they receive. Some parents spend months working with their pediatricians until they find the formula that agrees with their little ones' delicate digestive systems. Finally, as with breast-feeding, people give new moms advice on their decision to bottle-feed. People in the grocery store will criticize you for the cans of formula you have in your cart. Some fellow new moms who are nursing will all but demand to know why you are not. Or, this "advice" can be more subtle. It can be difficult for a new mom to hear another extol the virtues of breast milk when she is not breast-feeding.

Before discussing solutions to these challenges, it is essential to note that *Becoming a Calm Mom* advocates one thing about feeding, and one thing only: Babies must be fed to grow and thrive. Although a little more space may be devoted to breast-feeding (in response to what we learned from our survey respondents), the intention is not to tell moms that they should breast-feed. Rather, the intention is to let new moms feel comfortable with whatever choices they make about feeding their babies, whether breast-feeding, formula feeding, or a combination. A secondary goal is to help moms navigate the stress and anxiety that might prevent them from breast-feeding if this goal is important to them.

The Solutions

There are numerous ways to decrease the stress associated with feeding your baby. Consider the following tips.

IF YOU DECIDE TO BREAST-FEED, REMEMBER THAT IT OFTEN DOES NOT COME NATURALLY. In trying to feed your first baby, you have two completely clueless individuals trying to learn a rather complex skill. Mom has never breast-fed before, and baby has never even eaten before! The first time you try to nurse your baby, it is unlikely that he will just latch right on and start gulping down a delicious meal! It will take some practice for you to hold the baby correctly and for him to learn to latch on, stay awake for an entire meal, and not drink so much at once that he either chokes or spits up his whole meal when he is done. You also need to learn all sorts of new things, such as how to soothe sore breasts, operate a breast pump, and prevent large circles of milk from forming on your shirt every time you leave the house. This isn't easy stuff!

The most important thing is to *expect* that nursing can be challenging and get all the help you need as soon as possible. This means attending classes or reading books about breast-feeding before giving birth, seeking out the help of a lactation consultant in the hospital, and attending support groups for breast-feeding moms in your area after you get home. Many of the new moms in the Calm Moms Survey credited these kinds of resources with being able to persevere with breast-feeding when the going was tough.

Let's think back to our Calm Thinking strategy. Many new moms resist getting help with breast-feeding because they think it should come naturally or that they are doing something wrong or are defective in some way. These thoughts need some adjustments! Getting help means that you are doing everything you can to succeed at a very difficult and important task.

GET THE HELP YOU NEED. After you feel reassured that getting help is okay, the next concern is how to go about getting it. Many obstetricians and pediatricians can advise you on breast-feeding. In the first few months of your baby's life you will visit the pediatrician a lot, so discuss your concerns with your baby's doctor. If you have a pediatrician who is not particularly supportive of breast-feeding, you might want to find one who shares your views.

Another excellent source of help is a lactation consultant (see this book's "Resources for New Moms" section for information on finding one in your area). Lactation consultants help new moms navigate the many challenges that typically cause women to discontinue

75

breast-feeding. First, they provide education. Most women who have successfully supported a pregnancy can also successfully nurse a new baby. Healthy bodies are designed to make as much milk as our babies are taking in. When new moms worry that they are not making enough milk, they tend to supplement with formula and the result of this is decreased milk supply (it all comes down to the general rule of supply and demand). Lactation consultants reassure moms that they have enough milk and educate them on how to make sure their milk supply stays at a healthy level. Again, it is important to emphasize that *Becoming a Calm Mom* is not advocating a particular choice about feeding. However, if a new mom wants to breast-feed, a lactation consultant can correct misconceptions, thereby decreasing anxiety.

Lactation consultants also help new moms to get their babies to *latch on* correctly. Incorrect latching can lead to the pain that causes so many moms to stop nursing (and can lead to babies' not getting enough to eat). Lactation consultants can suggest remedies to soothe sore breasts, techniques to keep babies on task as they are eating (many newborns will doze off during feedings!), and perhaps most importantly, can help new moms develop reasonable expectations. For most moms, the initial discomfort associated with breast-feeding subsides quickly.

EXPECT THAT BOTTLE-FEEDING ALSO INVOLVES A LEARNING CURVE. There is an incorrect assumption that bottle-feeding is a simple endeavor compared with breast-feeding. In reality, there is a lot for new moms to learn when they choose to bottle-feed (e.g., what kind of formula and bottles to use, how to prepare bottles, how to clean bottles, how to burp the baby, etc.). And of course, babies need to learn to eat regardless of the method of food delivery! New moms should give themselves and their little ones a chance to catch on to the ins and outs of feeding and expect some challenges along the way.

As with nursing, get the help you need. Consult your pediatrician about what type of formula to use, how much to give your baby at each feeding, and whether to be concerned about spitting up or fussiness. Don't worry if you need to contact the pediatrician between visits; that is what he or she is there for! New moms worry that their pediatricians will think they are clueless, neurotic, or just a massive pain if they have lots of questions. They believe they should just know what to do to keep their baby well fed and healthy. However, getting help is not a sign of weakness. As with nursing, getting help means you are doing everything you can to succeed at a difficult and very important task—**feeding your baby.**

DON'T EQUATE FEEDING WITH YOUR SKILLS AS A MOM. There seems to be a general belief that moms who breast-feed are more dedicated to their infants than moms who formula feed. After all, breast-feeding is time-consuming, cannot be shared with others, and requires the mother to make a lot of lifestyle modifications (i.e., eating properly, drinking lots of fluids, not taking certain medications or drinking alcohol, regularly being with the baby or taking a breast pump when apart from the baby). Some people seem to think that bottle-feeding with formula is a cop out or makes new motherhood easier. These societal beliefs lead new moms to engage in a lot of negative self-talk if they are not able to breast-feed, or to an even greater degree if they can but choose not to breast-feed (or not to breast-feed exclusively).

The bottom line is that feeding a baby, whether with breast milk, formula, or both is a full-time job. Consider that when babies are first born, they eat every 2 to 3 hours which equates to about eight times a day. Babies can take up to 1 hour to finish each feeding. Before becoming a mom did you spend 8 hours a day at work? Well, your 8 hours have now been filled by your milk-guzzling bundle of joy! And although you may have worked at your old job from

9:00 a.m. to 5:00 p.m., your new job requires that you are on call around the clock and requires you to perform other duties, including numerous diaper changes, frequent soothing, and periodic entertaining. Whether you are spending your "free" time pumping breast milk or mixing bottles of formula, all new moms are working hard!

If you are giving yourself a hard time for choosing not to breast-feed or for choosing to supplement with formula, beware of the labels you might be assigning to yourself. Moms who make these choices often label themselves *lazy, selfish,* or *lacking commitment.* You don't need to take such nastiness—rather, engage in some Calm Thinking. Ask yourself, "Do you have any evidence that you are being lazy or selfish or that you lack commitment to your little one?" You can also ask, "Would you say these things about a friend who decided to supplement with formula, or who decided not to breast-feed at all?" Hopefully, you will conclude that becoming a mom is the busiest, most difficult, and least self-indulgent pursuit you will ever engage in! Furthermore, you should recognize that you would never say the terrible things you are saying to yourself to any of your friends. Consider the big picture of what it is to be a mom and come up with a calming thought to ground yourself when your thoughts threaten to get the better of you. A good one might be, "A lot more goes into being a great mom than what you feed your child."

FIGURE OUT YOUR MOTIVATIONS. As with all aspects of baby care, you must make a decision about feeding your baby that feels right to you and that is in line with your own values and lifestyle. After you have made a decision, identify one or two reasons why you made the choice. If you begin to waver or if another person's influence makes you feel guilty, remember your personal motives. Perhaps you decided to breast-feed because of the excellent immune properties of breast milk, because you were compelled by a study showing that breast-fed babies were less likely to grow into obese adults, or because you thought it would be easier than washing and preparing numerous bottles each day. Perhaps you decided to bottle-feed because you wanted your spouse to be involved in feeding the baby, because you wanted to be able to resume taking a medication that is contraindicated while nursing, or because you felt it would be more practical given the time frame within which you had to return to work. Remembering personal motives can be very grounding when doubt begins to intrude on a decision that you already made.

DON'T MAKE SNAP DECISIONS. Many moms who breast-feed recount a time when they almost gave up on it. Perhaps it was a day when they were struggling with discomfort or the day they went back to work and leaked milk through their shirt during a meeting with their (male) boss. Don't make decisions on these difficult days. Rather, wait a week or two, then reconsider. Often, after the discomfort is gone or a mom has established an effective pumping routine at work, all the doubts have disappeared. If after a week or two you still are considering discontinuing breast-feeding, use the Calm Mom Approach to Making Decisions. Rather than making a snap decision, this process will help you consider all your options, weigh the pros and cons of each, and arrive at a well thought-out decision.

DON'T LET ANXIETY GET IN THE WAY. As was evident in our Calm Moms Survey, breast-feeding can be fraught with anxiety. Is the baby getting enough to eat? Is she latched on correctly? Will I be able to get any rest before she needs to eat again? Anxiety can also interfere with bottle-feeding. Moms who bottle-feed their babies also worry about whether their little ones are eating the right amount. Regardless of the method of delivery, moms might become preoccupied with other issues that are stressing them out as they are feeding their babies. Babies can sense tension and will likely have more difficulty relaxing into the feeding routine if you are tense. Furthermore, anxiety can interfere with milk production in breast-feeding mothers.

The relaxation strategies introduced in chapter 3 are perfect to use while you are feeding your baby. Get the baby settled, close your eyes, and transport yourself to a relaxing place in your imagination. Do some breathing exercises. Turn on some calming music. As you release your anxiety and tension, it is likely that your baby will also relax and be able to focus on eating a good meal!

SLEEPING

The Facts

Knowing the facts about infant sleep can help new moms develop realistic expectations. According to Dr. Jodi Mindell, a pediatric sleep expert, there are significant differences between infant and adult sleep (personal communication, July 13, 2007; see also Dr. Mindell's book, *Sleeping Through the Night: How Infants, Toddlers, and Their Parents Can Get a Good Night's Sleep*, 2005). In contrast to adults, who typically have one long sleep period at night, babies have many brief sleep periods through the day and night. When babies are very young, they typically sleep every 2 to 4 hours through the day and night. At about 8 weeks, they will begin to sleep for longer stretches at night and stay awake longer during the day. Dr. Mindell explained that the average age at which babies sleep through the night is between 3 and 6 months old. Once this milestone is reached, however, 25% to 50% of 6- to 12-month-old babies still wake up during the night (even if they do not need anything, such as a meal). It is interesting that the 2004 Sleep in America survey, carried out by the National Sleep Foundation (see Mindell, 2005), revealed that 74%

of parents with children ages 0 to 10 would like to change something about their children's sleep.

The Challenges

Why are so many parents of babies and young children dissatisfied with their children's sleep? Perhaps because more than any other aspect of baby care, a baby's sleep pattern affects the parents' quality of life! According to Dr. James Maas (2008), a sleep expert at Cornell University, new parents lose 400 to 750 hours of sleep during their baby's first year. One mom who responded to the Calm Moms Survey wrote, "I honestly thought the lack of sleep would kill me." This might be a slight exaggeration, but there is no doubt that sleep deprivation has many negative effects. According to Dr. Maas, sleep deprivation can cause stress, anxiety, depressed mood, and irritability. It can affect our mental functioning, making it harder to concentrate, remember things, make decisions, and think logically. Sleep deprivation can even make us less able to use good coping skills to solve problems. Ironically, we face the effects of sleep deprivation at the same time we are confronting a myriad of challenges we never confronted before (namely, caring for a newborn). Clearly, the sleep deprivation that comes with having a new baby contributes directly to the stress experienced by new moms.

Another reason infant sleep patterns cause so much stress is that decisions about sleep are fraught with all sorts of value judgments. Some people favor co-sleeping, believing it is cruel to force infants and children to sleep on their own. Some favor having babies learn to sleep alone in their own rooms, seeing this as a crucial life skill that we use every day of our lives. When babies are crying, some people believe in going to check on them, whereas others believe in letting them cry it out. Some people hold staunchly to schedules and routines, and others believe that babies should set their own schedules according to their ever-changing needs. As with decisions about feeding, it is difficult to sort out what approach feels right to you. Furthermore, these conflicting opinions can become an issue in your home if you believe in one approach but your partner favors another.

The Solutions

Thankfully, there are many ways parents can ease the strain of their own sleep deprivation and the stress they experience about their baby's sleep patterns. Following are some tips to consider.

BE YOUR OWN BEHAVIOR THERAPIST. In chapter 2, I introduced the strategy of being your own behavior therapist. This strategy is crucially important in the arena of infant sleep. Babies are creatures of habit. From a very early age, they come to associate certain stimuli with going to sleep. It is their parents who establish these associations for them. Parents do all kinds of things to get their babies to sleep: driving around the block in the car, rocking in a comfortable chair, or lying down with the baby. Furthermore, parents introduce various sleep aids, from swaddling blankets to pacifiers to white noise machines. There is no doubt that all of these methods can help put your baby to sleep. However, Mindell (personal communication, 2007) suggests that parents consider how they would like bedtime to be when their baby is one year old and has a mind of her own! Think about whether you want to be rocking your 20-pound child to sleep every night or lugging the white noise machine to grandma's house to celebrate baby's first birthday.

If there is one essential thing for new moms to learn about infant sleep, it is this: **You better like whatever sleep routine you set up for your baby because you will be repeating it** *every time your baby goes to sleep.* Yes, that means at bedtime, naptime, and in the wee hours of the night.

Pairing some stimuli with sleep is important. Babies need to know the difference between awake and sleep time. Consistent sleep stimuli are the keys to accomplishing this goal. However, parents must give some thought to a routine that is easy to implement, efficient (i.e., no one wants a 2-hour bedtime routine!), and portable (for those visits to grandma).

Dr. Mindell (2005) also emphasized the importance of putting your baby down when he is drowsy but not yet asleep. Let's consider two scenarios to illustrate this essential point.

- Six-month-old Caroline plays with her mom and dad each evening until about 8:00 p.m. Then Mom takes Caroline up to her room, nurses her, and rocks her until she dozes off. She then gently puts her in her crib.
- Six-month-old Max plays with his mom and dad each evening until about 8:00 p.m. Then Mom, Dad, and Max go upstairs. Dad changes Max into his pajamas. Mom and Dad dim the lights in his room, and the family sits on the floor to read stories. After a few stories Max is quite drowsy, and Mom and Dad put him in bed. He grabs his favorite stuffed animal and drifts off into sleep.

Both babies have a nice bedtime routine with their parents. However, Caroline is put in her bed when she is already asleep; Max is put in his bed when he is drowsy. This seemingly subtle difference really matters when the babies wake up during the night (as all babies do) and need to get themselves back into deep sleep from a drowsy state. Caroline doesn't need to accomplish this on her own as part of her nighttime routine. Her mom helps her make the transition from drowsy to sleeping. For Max, progressing from drowsy to sleeping *is part of his nighttime routine.* This means that when Max wakes up in the middle of the night he can soothe himself back to sleep, whereas Caroline needs to be nursed and rocked by her very sleepy mom.

Many new parents are perplexed about when to initiate a bedtime routine. Dr. Mindell (2005) recommended doing so by the time your baby is 3 to 6 weeks old. This might seem like an odd suggestion, given that babies wake up and go back to sleep all day and night at this point. Yet, even babies this young are learning and forming important connections between stimuli and responses. Dr. Mindell suggested that in the early evening you should change your little one into pajamas, dim the lights, and read a story or sing a lullaby. Because most babies eat in the early evening, Dr. Mindell emphasized the importance of separating eating from sleeping. This last nighttime feeding can take place in a brighter, slightly louder environment (e.g., in the den with the lights on while you chat with the baby). Then, even if the baby has dozed off, it is okay to rouse him. Take him to his room and begin the bedtime routine of changing clothes, reading stories, and singing songs. In this way, you will be putting your little one to sleep when he is drowsy (but not asleep), so he learns how to get to sleep on his own.

CRYING ISN'T ALWAYS BAD. In the Calm Moms Survey, many new moms reported feeling a great deal of guilt when their babies cried as they were trying to get to sleep. They felt that they should rush in and do something. One mom eloquently wrote, "I found it very stressful when our son would cry for an hour or more as we tried all the tricks . . . feeding, rocking, swaddling, pacifier, music, etc . . . It seemed that nothing worked until he finally exhausted himself from crying for so long. I think the only thing we could have done differently was to relax during this nightly process. Looking back, I think it is normal that the baby cried at this time each night, but we were so stressed out during it that we worried that something was wrong with him or that we weren't doing something right."

It is important to remember that crying is not always indicative of something terrible; crying is discussed in greater detail later in this chapter. Babies cry when they are tired and overwhelmed, but crying at these times might also serve a function. It might help them blow off steam and drift off to sleep. Crying does not necessarily mean that your baby needs something or that you have done something wrong. In fact, when parents keep rushing in and trying a million different strategies, they can actual disturb the baby from his own natural progression into sleep. Do your sleep routine, then give the baby a chance to work his way into sleep on his own. It is fine to come back into his room to do a brief check (i.e., making sure he hasn't stuck an arm through the crib rails, or pulled something over his face), but don't fuss with him. Rather, engage in Calm Thinking to remind yourself that letting the baby cry does not mean you are a bad parent or that you have done something wrong. You can also do relaxation exercises. Go into another room (as far from the baby's room as possible) and calm yourself down. By the time you do so, you will often find that your baby has drifted off—and that you are more relaxed for bedtime too!

HAVE REASONABLE EXPECTATIONS. When I look back on my frustrations with my baby's sleep routine during the first 6 months of being a new mom, I now recognize that most of my trouble lay in unrealistic expectations. Being a behavior therapist (and having learned a lot from Dr. Mindell's book), I believed we were doing a pretty good job of establishing and sticking to a good bedtime routine. I think we were good about not running into the baby's room for every little peep and whimper. My problem was that I believed babies began sleeping through the night much sooner than they really do. When my baby took longer than I expected to sleep through the night, I blamed myself. I figured I must be doing something wrong (e.g., not making enough milk, not stimulating her enough during the day, making her room too dark or too light). As noted previously, babies typically sleep through the night between 3 and 6 months of age. Expecting a baby to sleep through the night after just a month or two is unrealistic and leads to undue stress.

DON'T ENGAGE IN SOCIAL COMPARISONS. One of the most common questions people ask new moms is, "Is she sleeping through the night yet?" It would be nice if people could think of a more interesting question to ask, such as, "Has she smiled yet?" or "Does she like going outside for walks?" For some reason, everyone seems preoccupied by the "sleeping through the night" issue. It might be that this question serves as a subtle way of asking how a new mom is doing, because most parents remember how grueling those first sleep-deprived months were. Although this question might be asked with the best intentions, it can be irksome for parents whose babies have not reached this milestone.

I was one of the easily irked people because my baby took longer to sleep through the night than most. One day we were having a play date with friends who had a baby who was younger than ours. They told us that their little guy was sleeping through the night. My husband politely asked, "What do you mean by that exactly?" It turns out that our friends stayed up until 1 a.m. each night. They began rocking their little one around midnight and after he fell asleep in their arms, they transferred him to his crib. This rocking and transferring process often required a few repetitions because he would wake up when he was moved. After he was settled at about 1:00 a.m., he slept peacefully in his crib until 6:00 a.m., when he was ready to eat.

My husband was onto something: What did people really mean when they said their baby slept through the night? When we started asking, we came to realize that people define this milestone in different ways. We defined it as our daughter going to bed at 8:00 p.m. after her nighttime routine and not hearing from her again until about 6:00 a.m. No nighttime feedings. No emergency pacifier replacements. No pats on the head. We discovered that our criteria were more stringent than others' and more important, we learned to stop comparing our baby with other infants. Incidentally, since our little one started to sleep through the night (as defined by us!), she has been a stellar sleeper. We still follow an age-appropriate modification of our original nighttime routine, and she waves to us and says "bye" when we leave her room. Barring the occasional middle of the night stomach bug, we don't see her again until morning. Okay, that's not exactly true—we do come in and gaze at her before we go to bed, but that just doesn't count!

TAKE CARE OF YOURSELF. Some respondents to the Calm Moms Survey were particularly stressed about their own sleep deprivation. As already noted, this is one reason infant sleep is such a big issue. Unless you have chronic insomnia or had to endure a particularly grueling sleep schedule because of your work, you are unlikely to have experienced the effects of chronic sleep deprivation at any other time in your life. And let's face it, these effects are brutal.

With this in mind, it is essential that new moms try to take care of themselves as best they can. In fact, when I asked Dr. Mindell for words of wisdom on infant sleep, she said that parents must make their own sleep a priority. First, figure out whether you can share the burden of night feedings. Some moms find that having help even on one or two nights of the week makes a huge difference. For example, your partner could take care of the nighttime feedings on weekends, giving you 2 solid nights of sleep each week.

The second essential component of taking care of yourself is to nap when the baby naps. This is advice new moms are given all the time but rarely take. There is so much to do when the baby naps! Why would anyone waste this precious time by sleeping? There is a way to strike a balance. Babies nap multiple times a day. Try to nap during one of their naps. If you are not good at napping, at least sit down and do something totally relaxing such as reading a book or calling a friend. Then, during the baby's other naps you can catch up on necessary chores. Use your Calm Thinking strategies to stop criticizing yourself for taking care of Mom!

Third, if sleep deprivation is getting to be too much for you and you see no way out, consider other options. If you do not have much family support, it might be worth hiring a college student to help you out one day per week so you can get some rest. If you are committed to breast-feeding exclusively, it might be worth investing in a breast pump so you can express some milk and have your partner take one feeding each night. It can be hard to ask for help, but even a few extra hours of sleep can make you feel like a new person.

Some new moms have trouble falling back to sleep after feeding their babies or find it impossible to nap during the day. If this is true for you, try the relaxation strategies introduced in chapter 3. Also, be aware of your thoughts when you are trying to get to sleep; negative thoughts can easily come when you are lying in bed, bone-tired, but unable to get to sleep. Engage in Calm Thinking; after you are in a clearer state of mind, it should be easier to drift off. Finally, be your own behavior therapist. Are there stimuli in the environment preventing you from sleeping? Are you trying to battle sleep deprivation with vast amounts of caffeine? If so, cut back. Replace caffeine with a high-energy snack or a brisk walk around the block. If you want to nap during the day turn off the phone ringer, e-mail, TV, and lights. At night, many parents become preoccupied with the sounds of their babies. If constant attention to breathing and every little peep is keeping you up, turn down the baby monitor; if your baby is sleeping in your room, consider moving him to his own room. When a baby needs something, you will hear it!

Finally, reassure yourself that babies become better sleepers every single day. With each passing month, moms and dads will get more sleep too. If you establish a good sleep routine and apply it consistently, you and your baby will eventually sleep through the night and wake up feeling well rested in the morning.

CRYING

The Facts

According to Roberta Golinkoff and Kathy Hirsch-Pasek (1999), experts in infant language development, "One of the first things parents notice is that babies cry . . . and cry . . . and cry" (p. 20). They explain that babies cry anywhere from 30 minutes to 3 hours each day. Crying reaches its peak frequency when a baby is 2 months old and begins to decline from there.

When your baby cries, do you feel uncomfortable? Do you notice changes in your body? If you noticed physiological changes, you are perceptive and you are accurate! When babies cry, both men and women experience uncomfortable physiological changes that are consistent with distress. These changes include increased alertness, circulation, blood pressure, and respiration. In other words, your body reacts to crying the same way it would react if you were being chased by a bear through the woods!

In addition to physiological changes, a baby's cry has a powerful effect on a parent's thoughts. When babies cry, you immediately assume that something is wrong. This makes you behave as though a bear is chasing you (and your baby!) through the woods— dashing around furiously and trying anything you can think of to calm down this anguished little person. In reality, crying rarely means something is terribly wrong. According to T. Berry Brazelton, an internationally recognized expert on child development, "Crying is a universal, adaptive behavior and a baby's most effective form of communication" (2006, p. 231). Crying can communicate any number of states including hunger, boredom, pain, and exhaustion. Cry-

89

ing can also serve a function beyond communication. If you had a stressful day at work and want to wind down before bed, you might go for a walk or read a book. A baby cannot do these things. She might cry as her way to blow off steam. Crying is one of the few things babies can do independently when they are born (and boy, can they do it well!). It is always a good idea to discuss crying with your pediatrician if it seems that your baby is crying excessively. At the same time, it is important to remember that crying is rarely indicative of an all-out catastrophe!

The Challenges

Many respondents to the Calm Moms Survey described frustrations with soothing their crying babies. Knowing how to respond to crying is difficult for many reasons. The most significant reason may be that crying is mysterious—why the baby is crying is rarely crystal clear. Furthermore, there are no simple rules for soothing a crying baby. After you have attended to obvious culprits such as hunger or wet diapers, babies often continue crying. One mom wrote, "I was always trying to find the 'miracle cure' that would calm his crying. Unfortunately, I never discovered the 'miracle;' it was always something different every day." This uncertainty feeds into feelings of self-doubt. Is the baby sick? Is the baby unhappy? Am I doing something wrong? There may be nothing else that makes you question your skill as a parent as much as a screaming, red-faced infant!

Finally—and let's be honest—crying can be infuriating. When it first begins, we feel badly for our babies and want to do whatever we can to help them. However, after we attend to the obvious needs and the crying continues, many moms feel like asking, "Well, baby, what the heck do you want from me now?" These feelings of frustration only exacerbate doubts about our skills as mothers.

The Solutions

Let's consider some tips for dealing with the anxiety associated with a crying baby.

CRYING CAN MEAN LOTS OF THINGS. Crying can be indicative of many different things. There is no doubt that when a baby begins to cry, we should attend to his or her obvious needs as soon as possible. Is he hungry? Does she need a diaper change? Is something irritating him, like a bright light shining in his eyes? A mom can gain a great sense of satisfaction from identifying one of these obvious needs, resolving it, and seeing her baby calm right down.

As a new mom, I often forgot two other related reasons for crying: exhaustion and overstimulation. When my baby was a few weeks old, I learned from Dr. Mindell's book (2005) that babies need to go back to sleep 2 hours after they wake up. This was new to me. This essentially means that new babies eat (which can take a full hour), hang out and play for a bit, and then really need to get some rest. Particularly when they are tired, babies will also cry from overstimulation. When they begin to cry, parents think they want attention and amusement. However, being talked to and having toys dangled in front of him or her can bother a baby even more! If you have fed, changed, played with your baby, and given her the once over to ensure that nothing is hurting her, remember that she might just be screaming out for a break and a rest.

Beyond these essentials, babies cry for reasons that remain completely unclear to their poor, stressed out parents. It is important for new moms and dads to remember that crying does not always mean something is wrong with the baby or that they are doing something that is causing their babies to cry despite their best efforts at soothing.

Remembering that babies cry for many reasons is an exercise in Calm Thinking. If your baby is crying and you catch yourself thinking,

"I'm not helping him," or "He's unhappy," or "He's sick," replace these thoughts. Try thinking, "Maybe he's blowing off some steam," or "Maybe he's telling the world that he's exhausted and wants to get some sleep . . . after all, it's been a whole two hours since his last nap!" After negative assumptions about crying are stopped, moms can learn to accept that babies cry (a lot), and that is okay.

A CALM MOM EQUALS A CALM BABY. After you move into a stance of acceptance—"Babies cry, and that's okay"—you can enjoy your daily routine with the baby instead of being paralyzed by fear and anxiety every time your baby whimpers! As already noted, you should attend to your baby's needs when he cries. You would not want to sit around in a dirty diaper, and neither does he! But if you have tended to the obvious factors and he is still crying, work on calming *yourself* instead of calming him.

Sitting at home with a screaming baby is a great time to try relaxation exercises. All the exercises in chapter 3 can be done with a baby in your arms (just make sure not to squish the baby as you tense your muscles if you try the muscle relaxation exercise!). As the baby feels your tension floating away, he is likely to relax too.

Other relaxation strategies designed for you can calm babies too. If we were having one of those days of unending crying, I would pop my little one into her stroller and we would head out for a walk. At first I was definitely doing this for my own benefit, as I always enjoyed walking and taking in all the sounds and smells of nature. Yet I quickly learned that my daughter loved these walks too. I don't know if it was the motion, change in scenery, fresh air, or chirping birds, but something about those walks lulled her to sleep on even her crankiest days. In inclement weather, try going for a walk at your local mall.

Other ways to calm yourself include taking a hot bath or shower, turning on nice music, or doing a yoga or exercise video. Again, you can do all these things with your baby. You can keep an eye on her, and the exact stimuli that calm you down might calm her too. Remember, it is also fine to put her in her crib and go somewhere else in the house to do your own thing. Because overstimulation and exhaustion make babies upset, your little one might settle down more easily in her own bed than when barraged by lights, funny yoga music, and the sight of mom contorting herself into all sorts of weird positions.

It is important to directly address the issue of frustration. When babies cry incessantly, moms can really begin to lose their cool. This can lead to feelings of guilt. It feels wrong to be frustrated with an innocent, helpless little baby. Moms start to berate themselves, believing they should not be feeling these emotions. Some also worry that they will become so frustrated that they will yell at or even harm the baby. Experiencing these thoughts occasionally is completely normal. In the appendix these thoughts are discussed in more detail to help you differentiate normal thoughts from those that warrant professional help. Feel free to jump ahead now to the appendix if you are experiencing harm-related thoughts that are extremely frequent and intense.

If these thoughts arise only occasionally and are fleeting, rest assured they are completely normal. New babies can be frustrating and can bring out unusual thoughts and strong feelings we never imagined we would have. At times like these, the best thing to do is to put the baby in a safe place (his bed is probably the best bet) and take a breather. Take a quick shower. Go into another room in your house and do something relaxing, or call someone to whom you can vent for a few minutes. If it's a really hard day, call someone you trust to watch the baby for an hour or two so you can have a break and recharge your batteries.

Be mindful of your thinking at these times. When moms feel they need a break, negative thoughts often come quickly and furiously: "I'm a failure at this," "I am sure other moms don't get as frustrated as I do," "I *should* be able to handle this better than

I am." Remember, the Calm Thinking steps are question your thoughts, answer the questions, and come up with a calming statement. Good questions in response to these thoughts are, "How would I define someone who has failed as a mother? Do I fit this definition?" "Do I know with certainty that other moms don't get frustrated?" "If my best friend were having a day like this, would I expect her to handle it better than I am right now?" Answering these questions might lead a new mom to conclude, "Being a new mom is a really hard job. Recognizing that I *need* a break is actually a sign of success, not failure. Taking a brief break will make me a better, more patient mom when I get back."

BE YOUR OWN BEHAVIOR THERAPIST. As you get to know your baby and your baby gets to know about the world, you can do some sleuthing to figure out what methods tend to soothe her. I have selected the word *tend* here for a reason—as noted at the beginning of this section, what soothes a baby one day might fail completely the next. With that said, you can succeed at being your own behavior therapist. Does your baby like to be swaddled, or does she prefer to have her limbs free? Does she like a pacifier, or does she spit it out? When she is fussy, does she like to be rocked (e.g., in a swing), does she like bouncing (in a bouncy seat), or does she just like stillness (laying on her back on a mat on the floor)? Most babies will not like a soothing method the first time you use it. Try it several times and then decide. You will arrive at strategies that work. Try to keep it simple and try not to overwhelm yourself or the baby with too many strategies.

REMEMBER THAT CALM MOM STRATEGIES WORK IN PUBLIC, TOO. As bad as crying is in the privacy of your home, it is more difficult to deal with in public places. Dealing with a crying baby in a restaurant, the grocery store, on an airplane, or even at a friend's house is difficult for

94

two reasons. On a simple level, you have less access to your favorite soothing tools. If the baby swing is your surefire soothing tool at home, you are out of luck on an airplane. More important, we worry about the judgments of others when our babies cry in public. All the miserable things we say to ourselves sound even worse when we assume they are passing through the minds of strangers (or friends). We assume other people think we are terrible, incompetent parents because we can't soothe our babies.

A few strategies work in these situations. First, you can engage in calm thinking. Try this exercise the next time you are in a public place and feel worried about others' judgments. Assume that there are 100 people around you. How many have even noticed that your baby is crying? Remember that your baby's crying is louder and more upsetting to you than to anyone else around you. Some people simply won't be close enough to notice. And some people might be so lost in their own thoughts that a crying baby is insignificant background noise. Let's imagine that at your neighborhood restaurant, 50 out of 100 people don't even notice that your baby is raising a ruckus.

This leaves you with 50 people who notice your baby's crying. Of these 50 people, how many do you think give your crying baby a second thought beyond, "Hmmm, I hear a baby crying?" Perhaps 20 people have this thought but move on to other thoughts that have nothing to do with babies or your skills as a parent. We are now down to 30 people who (a) notice your baby crying and (b) give it a second thought. It is time to consider the probable thoughts of these people. Are all 30 thinking negative thoughts about you and your baby? Probably not. Here are some possible thoughts:

- I feel sorry for that woman. I remember how hard it was to soothe my baby when he got like that.
- Poor little guy. Maybe it's too loud in here for him.
- I wonder if he's hungry.

- Too bad that woman and her husband couldn't get a babysitter tonight. She looks as though she needs a break.
- Cute little guy!

These are a few examples, but they highlight two important points. Of the people who notice that your baby is crying and give it more than a passing thought, the way they interpret the situation will vary greatly. Some may feel sorry for you, some may feel sorry for the baby, and some won't have much reaction beyond thinking your baby is cute. Of our 30 people, a few will undoubtedly have negative thoughts about you. They might think that the best place for a baby is at home or that you do not have any idea how to soothe this angry beast. Okay, fine. Everyone is entitled to his or her opinions.

The question to consider with these people is, "Do I care?" Do you care if a few curmudgeonly people believe that a baby should be home crying in his or her own nursery? Do you care if a complete stranger is questioning your parenting abilities? After you consider these questions you might realize that opinions held by complete strangers are not important to you and have no relationship to the kind of person you are.

Obviously, you are not going to perform the *What do 100 people think?* exercise every time you are out with a crying infant. Rather, you can lapse right into a calming thought. Remind yourself, "This is way more noticeable to me than to anyone else. I am not a mind reader. Some people probably feel badly for me and some people are probably angry with me. But it really is of no consequence whatsoever." Then get on with your day.

Relaxation exercises also work well in public places. I spent many an airplane trip trying to soothe my baby while zoning off in my mind to my favorite place. By closing my eyes I was able to block out the glares of annoyed seatmates, and as I relaxed my daughter tended to relax as well.

One point to keep in mind with respect to public places is to *avoid avoidance*. Many new moms avoid going out because they are afraid of how they will deal with the inevitable crying infant. The problem with avoidance is that it can bring on other problems— loneliness, isolation, boredom, and a feeling of ineffectiveness if nothing gets done besides caring for the baby. The more you go out and are forced to deal with public displays of crying, the easier it will get. You will come to realize that most people don't notice or care and that those who do sometimes offer wonderful suggestions, rather than harsh critiques.

FILLING THE DAY

The Facts

Although the early weeks of parenthood are mostly occupied with feeding, sleeping, soothing, and changing, the time will soon come when babies need entertaining. As babies begin to sleep for longer stretches at night they stay awake for longer periods during the day. There are no rules about how to amuse a baby, and there are no sta- tistics available on what the average parent does to fill a baby's day. This elusiveness can lead to anxiety in new moms.

The Challenges

One respondent to our Calm Moms Survey spoke clearly about this anxiety: "I was very surprised and a little embarrassed about what I found most difficult. It was finding activities during my baby's awake time. Surely playing with your baby should be the easier part, right? I was worried that I was not stimulating her enough and then I wor- ried about whether I was providing developmentally appropriate activities." In other words, as with discussions on most aspects of baby care, figuring out how to amuse a baby can bring out a mother's feelings of incompetence.

The Solutions

Consider these tips on the topic of filling the day:

BABIES DON'T NEED ANYTHING FANCY. Many new parents deal with their anxiety about entertaining their little ones by buying loads of toys. Early on, however, babies don't need a lot. Pediatricians encourage you to give your baby some *tummy time* (placing your baby on his or her tummy to play) each day so he or she can strengthen the muscles that are necessary to eventually sit up, crawl, and walk. There are fancy mats on which babies can do tummy time, but all you really need is a nice soft blanket. You can also place little stuffed toys or rattles around the baby so he or she can begin to practice reaching for things.

In the first few months the baby's greatest entertainment will be you! During periods of alertness, sit with her to have a chat. Some moms express concern that they don't know what to say. Say anything! Tell her a story about how you and daddy met. Tell her about the weather outside. Start reading books to her as soon as she is born.

Babies are entertained by all the basics of daily living. Sit on the floor next to your baby to fold the laundry when she is doing tummy time. Bring her with you to check your e-mail and read some of the messages out loud. Put her in a swing in the kitchen when you are making dinner and explain to her what you are making. Check out the Internet for age-appropriate games such as peekaboo (the Web site http://www.Babycenter.com has great ideas; see "Resources for New Moms"). None of these activities involves fancy toys or any skill on your part. Simply being with you, hearing your voice, and seeing your face is entertainment enough for a wee baby.

As babies get older they enjoy toys more and more. Keep in mind that you will get bored with their toys months before they do. We had a brightly colored play mat with overhanging toys that our little girl played on every day for the first 6 months of her life. We felt guilty about not providing her with more variety. But each morning as we put her down on her mat she was so excited that you might think we had purchased a brand new toy overnight! As a newborn, she loved looking at her face in the mirror affixed to the mat. Later, she loved to gaze up at the little animals. Then she learned to reach for the animals. For her developing brain, that toy offered new and exciting adventures every day. Recently we pulled out the mat for a friend who was visiting with a newborn baby. At age 2, our daughter still loved that mat. But this time she started to tell us the names of all the animals!

The play mat taught us that babies enjoy consistency, but as they develop, a single toy is played with in many different ways. Furthermore, babies tend to enjoy simple things. Your baby will probably go through a phase when the most exciting thing to him or her is the tag on the side of a toy or even the tag on the side of a dishtowel or burp cloth. So much for buying fancy toys!

ENJOY THE MOMENT RATHER THAN WORRY ABOUT WHAT'S NEXT. Has this happened to you? Your baby is lying on his play mat, happily grabbing for his little animal friends and your mind is fixated on what you are going to do in 20 minutes when he gets bored and fussy. Perhaps you are thinking, "What if I can't figure out what to do next?", and "What if he gets so fussy that I can't calm him down?" Quickly following are often thoughts about one's competence as a mother, "I don't know how to entertain him," and "It seems as though other moms always know what to do to keep their babies happy." Thoughts such as these are a cue to use Calm Mom strategies.

Certainly, Calm Thinking at a moment like this would be help-ful. Perhaps the most important tip is to simply **be in the moment.** When you notice your mind rushing ahead to what is going to hap-pen at 9:00 a.m., noon, and 3:00 p.m., catch yourself and ask, "Is this a helpful thing for me to be thinking about?" My hope is that you would answer *no* and shift your focus to the present moment. By worrying about what comes next, you just missed out on the pleasure of watching your baby enjoy his animal friends and develop a new skill (reaching). At times like this the best thing to do is to let the baby take the lead. Wait until he starts to get fussy. Then decide what comes next.

IT'S OKAY TO FEEL BORED. One goal of *Becoming a Calm Mom* is to be frank and honest. So here it is. Staying home with a new baby can be boring, no matter how much you love your baby. One new mom who responded to the Calm Moms Survey wrote, "The boredom of a newborn is mind-numbing." Before you call the authorities, let me assure you this woman is a super mom. She was just being honest about her experience. The problem arises when new moms progress from the thought "I am bored" to, "How dare I say that? I have wanted a baby forever," or "I don't deserve to be a mom," or "I am just being selfish." A few days of thoughts like this and even the hardiest mom might start to feel down in the dumps.

The Calm Thinking strategy involves the importance of accept-ing all thoughts and emotions and resisting the temptation to label them *good* or *bad*. The thought, "I am bored" is just a thought. It is as valid to your experience as a new mom as, "Wow, that was fun." You might have had the "Wow, that was fun" thought 20 minutes earlier and thought nothing of it, but that "I am bored" thought can throw new moms for a loop.

In addition to using Calm Thinking strategies (e.g., using the calming thought, "It is okay to be bored from time to time. It's a common feeling. It means nothing about my skills as a mom"), be your own behavior therapist. New moms often become bored because they are focused on having what they perceive to be a "baby-friendly" day. New moms should ask themselves, "What can I add into my day so I am not bored?" There are many things moms can do to satisfy themselves that are also nice for babies. For many new moms, simply getting out of the house helps. Going for a walk or running errands, although seemingly mundane, can give you a real lift. It is also fine to do some things for yourself. Do you want to pick up new books at the bookstore? Get a haircut? Get your favorite sandwich at the place you bought lunch before the baby came along? Go for it! Your baby will enjoy the fresh air and will like having new things to look at besides your living room ceiling. Finally, social interaction is one of the best ways to quell new mom boredom and provide a baby with opportunities to socialize too. Meeting up with other new moms or visiting a relative or friend can ensure a satisfying day for you and your little one.

BABIES DON'T NEED COMPANY EVERY MINUTE OF THE DAY. One issue that concerns new moms is the degree to which they should play with their babies. If baby is on his play mat, does mom need to be lying right there on the floor playing with him? Or can she be bustling around in the same room making dinner? Moms can get stressed out if they think they always need to be interacting with their babies during every waking moment. Yes, you should get down on the floor and play with your little one. Sitting in a chair and watching is not the same thing. Little babies who cannot see very far or move around much might not even notice you are there if you are not right next to them! You can't reasonably expect to play with your baby every moment he or she is awake. It is okay if you spend some parts of your day making dinner, calling a friend, or sitting and reading a book nearby while your baby is playing. This will result in two outcomes—you will be a more satisfied mom because you will have time to accomplish things that make you feel good, and your baby will learn independence skills that will be important for the rest of his or her life.

One controversial topic is television. Can moms watch TV while their little ones are present? Can children's television programs be considered an activity in a baby's day? These are complex questions, and this book doesn't answer them. However, we should consider a few important points. On the basis of the available research, the AAP does not recommend television for children younger than 2 years. The reality, however, is that many children are exposed to television before their second birthdays.

To help guide decisions about television viewing, moms can consider a few factors. First, quantity is undoubtedly important. If baby is exposed to 20 minutes of TV a day, this is probably less harmful than many hours a day. If a baby is plopped in front of a TV for many hours a day, it means they are not being spoken or read to, they are not playing, and they are not getting out to see new things or meet new people. All these activities are essential to a baby's development—TV is not. Second, quality is important. Putting the baby in front of adult television programs is useless and possibly harmful (particularly if the program is loud, fast, or violent). If you choose to expose your child to TV, find something as age-appropriate as you can. Finally, do not be unrealistic about what television is providing for your child. Be realistic and honest. If you put your baby in front of a video for 20 minutes so you can make dinner, admit that your goal is to make dinner. The video is providing a benefit for *you*. Yes, some videos seem to have a calming effect on little ones. That's great. But if you are using videos because you think they make your baby smarter, realize that there is little scientific evidence that videos or TV provide any educational benefit for very young children. This doesn't mean you should not use them. It just means that you should take them for what they are—a little break for you and some quiet time for your baby.

BABY DEVELOPMENT

The Facts

As noted earlier, none of the moms in the Calm Moms Survey reported feeling stressed about their baby's development. However, I found from my work with clients and interactions with my new mom friends that new moms do worry about this important issue.

It would be impossible in a brief paragraph to get into the intricacies of normal and abnormal infant development. The best source of information on these topics is your pediatrician. During regular visits your pediatrician should ask questions about developmental milestones, observe your baby in action (e.g., by putting her on her tummy to see if she can hold her head up), and educate you about what to expect next. Pediatricians know exactly what to look for in terms of developmental problems.

New parents can also look to reputable sources such as the AAP (see "Resources for New Moms" at the end of this book for more information on their Web site and publications) to learn about developmental milestones and when they can expect their children to meet them. It is essential that new parents understand that babies accomplish developmental milestones within age *ranges*. As an example, the AAP states that by 12 months, babies should be able to walk holding onto furniture and stand momentarily without support and *may* walk two or three steps without support. By 18 months, babies should be able to walk without support. This means that it is *normal* to begin to walk any time from before 12 months all the way up to 18 months. A baby who walks before her or his first birthday and a baby who walks at 18 months are both normal; they just accomplished this developmental milestone at the extreme ends of the normal distribution. Knowing this simple fact eases a lot of anxiety for new parents.

The Challenges

All parents want their babies to grow into healthy, well-functioning adults. Therefore, it makes sense that parents are attentive to their children's development and concerned that development progresses normally. Concerns about development may be more salient with first babies because parents have little or no grounds for comparison. For example, I had no idea that newborn babies could not make eye contact during their first few months of life. I was taken aback when we would talk to our baby and she would gaze into the distance. It wasn't until I saw lots of other babies doing the same thing that I realized it was completely normal!

Although spending time with other babies who are the same age as your own can ease some concerns about development, others might be exacerbated. Because babies meet developmental milestones within age *ranges,* you will see other babies meet these milestones before your baby. Seeing a baby who is the same age as yours roll across a room when your baby has not even attempted to roll over can make any new mom experience a little flutter of worry.

The Solutions

The overwhelming majority of babies develop normally. This does not mean, however, that parents don't worry about development. Here are some tips for managing your stress.

DON'T COMPETE IN THE BABY OLYMPICS. As noted, comparing your baby with others is a double-edged sword. On one hand, watching other babies who are the same age as yours can be a helpful way of knowing whether your little one is doing what he is supposed to be doing. On the other hand, because milestones are reached within age ranges, there will be times when your baby lags behind others. All babies do not magically start walking during the exact same month of life.

Rather than worrying when a friend's baby reaches a particular milestone before your child, think about the statement, "milestones are reached within age *ranges.*" Knowing this can help you to calm down. Although it might be reasonable to be concerned if your baby is 20 months old and has not started to walk (i.e., she passed the upper end of normal and has not accomplished a particular milestone), it is less reasonable to be concerned if your baby is 13 months old and has not yet started to walk.

Rather than compare your baby with others, compare your baby with . . . your baby! Is your baby doing more this month than he did last month? Is a skill that he accomplished last month more finely honed this month? These types of questions, in conjunction with regular visits to a pediatrician who is objective and well-educated, are the best ways to judge whether your baby is developing appropriately.

ENJOY EACH STAGE. Parents are often so preoccupied with the next developmental milestone that they don't enjoy the developmental stage their baby has already reached. I will share a slightly embarrassing personal example here, one that may be typical of new parents. At 9 months, our first child looked as though she really wanted to crawl. She would see a toy across the room and look at it with longing. Her problem was that she could not get herself from her tummy into a crawling position. We decided to coach her along. We would lift her from her tummy into a crawling position, only to have her plop right back down. My sweet, athletic husband would even demonstrate to her how to crawl. She would simply lie there and giggle at him. After a few days, Coach Gary and Coach Deborah backed off. We saw we were making no progress at all. A month later, our daughter started to crawl on her own. She got herself into a crawling position in a totally different way than we had been showing her. We showed her how to get into position from her tummy, but she would throw herself forward from a sitting position instead. Clearly, we were encouraging her to crawl before she was ready *and* showing her how to do it in a way that did not make sense to her. Meanwhile, for those few days of silly coaching we missed out on what she was doing right then. From then on, we decided to focus on the moment and let her learn and develop in her own, unique way.

Another thing parents say is, "I wish he could walk," or "I wish he could feed himself." Again, with this thinking ahead, you miss out on what your children are doing right now. Enjoy the days that you put your baby down somewhere and he stays right there! It is incredibly exciting when your child learns to walk, but it means that life becomes much busier and more worrisome as he darts all over the house getting into mischief. Try to enjoy feeding your little one; although it is certainly great when your child can hold her own bottle, reaching this milestone means no more cuddles during feedings. There is no denying that each new stage is more exciting than the one before, but be sure to savor each as it is happening, rather than focusing on what is coming next.

BE PROACTIVE IF YOU HAVE CONCERNS. The message of the previous two tips was for parents to become less preoccupied with developmental issues. Let your children develop on their own schedule and enjoy each stage as it is happening. Some children, however, do experience developmental problems. Parents might begin to sense that there is a problem when their child repeatedly misses developmental milestones (i.e., passes the high end of *normal* without accomplishing tasks). Sometimes it is just a feeling that all is not right. Brazelton writes, "As the front line in children's health and well-being, parents should respect their own observations and intuition" (2006, p. 243).

Some parents are so daunted by having a child who might have challenges that they don't want to voice their concerns out loud. They mentally reassure themselves that their child is just a little slower than others and will catch up. Other parents do voice concerns but find others downplaying them. Pediatricians, friends, and grandparents might provide undue reassurance.

The bottom line is that the intuition of a parent—*even a first time parent*—is often right. You are your child's only advocate, and because early intervention can be essential for infants and toddlers, it is vital to pay attention to your concerns and do something about them. Schedule a longer visit with your pediatrician if you want him or her to more carefully assess and discuss your concerns. Ask your pediatrician for a referral to a developmental pediatrician who is a specialist in infant and child development. All 50 states offer free early intervention programs for children with developmental problems, and pediatricians are the best people to get you initially connected with these services.

GERMS AND ILLNESS

The Facts

There is nothing more frightening to a new parent than having a sick infant. Although many books discuss common childhood illnesses, I found that few discussed parental *anxiety* about germs and illnesses. Therefore, I interviewed Dr. Madeleine Weiser, a board-certified pediatrician in the Philadelphia area who has more than 20 years of experience in this field (personal communication, July 19, 2007).

When I asked her for one "pearl of wisdom" to share with new parents on the topic of germs and illnesses, she said, "For the most part, children are amazingly well and resilient."

Dr. Weiser described what parents can expect regarding illness in the first year of life. She explained that in the first 6 months of life, babies are typically healthy. New babies and their moms spend a great deal of their time at home, and parents are typically cautious about making people wash their hands before picking up their baby. Babies who have siblings and babies who spend a lot of time with other babies (e.g., in day care) tend to suffer more illnesses during the first 6 months of life.

As babies grow and moms become more comfortable with taking them out, illnesses become more frequent. Babies typically come down with coughs, colds, and gastrointestinal bugs. After babies are 6 months of age, these illnesses are rarely serious and are usually more upsetting to parents than to the babies themselves (of course, you should always consult your pediatrician if you have concerns). As babies become more mobile in the second half of their first year of life, it is also likely that parents will be faced with their babies' first (hopefully minor) *boo-boo*.

The Challenges

Why are health issues so challenging for new parents? On the most basic level, the challenge comes from your little ones not being able to talk! If they seem under the weather, you can't just ask them to tell you what is wrong or what they need. Second, health-related issues can be quite elusive. One day, your baby might not seem "right." Particularly as a first-time parent, it is impossible to determine if this feeling amounts to nothing, is indicative of something minor (that the baby is getting a tooth or developing a cold), or is a signal of a major catastrophe (that the baby has a life-threatening illness). This uncertainty leads to conflicting emotions. On one hand, first-time parents often doubt their intuition ("What do I know? I've never had a baby before."). On the other hand, new parents are terribly afraid of making mistakes. Depending on the parent's personality, these conflicting emotions can either lead to a reluctance to seek help ("The doctor will think I am a nut for bringing the baby in") or an overreliance on help (e.g., seeking undue reassurance from doctors and others that the baby will be okay).

The other reason health-related matters are so difficult is that parents tend to blame themselves for any sniffle or boo-boo that befalls their babies. Consider a mom who is itching to get out of the house and takes the baby to the mall. The next day, the baby comes down with a terrible cold. A new mom may end up feeling guilty and label herself *selfish* because, of course, it was she who wanted to go to the mall, not her baby! Similarly, consider a mom whose baby rolls off the changing table when she bends down to pick up a dropped diaper. Following a scary episode such as this, moms assign negative labels to themselves, ranging from *incompetent* to *careless* to *undeserving*. Your baby is completely dependent on you, meaning that when anything happens to them, you feel responsible—whether or not this is realistic.

The Solutions

Consider the following solutions if you find yourself worrying about your baby's health.

TRUST YOUR INTUITION. New parents often doubt their intuition about their babies' health and well-being. In many cases, the concern underlying their doubts is negative evaluation from others. New moms worry that if they go to the pediatrician because of a feeling or because of something seemingly minor, the pediatrician (or other people in their lives) will label them as neurotic or stupid. Such beliefs call for Calm Thinking. Moms can ask themselves, "What's the worst thing that could happen?" The worst thing that could happen is that Mom ends up being wrong and the baby turns out to be perfectly healthy! Sounds like a pretty good outcome to me. When I interviewed Dr. Weiser (personal communication, July 19, 2007), she emphasized the importance of *dialogue* between pediatricians and parents. She made clear that pediatricians should take all parents' concerns seriously and should make time to engage in a discussion about these concerns. She pointed out that if pediatricians are dogmatic and make all dialogue one-sided and judgmental, parents should consider switching to another doctor who will be more respectful and responsive to their concerns.

ALWAYS WEIGH COSTS AND BENEFITS. Many new moms stay close to home and limit visitors when their babies are very young in an effort to prevent illness. Similarly, new moms often consider concerns about illnesses as they make decisions about returning to work and placing their little ones in child care. One mom who responded to our survey wrote, "As my baby was born in the fall he was not old enough for the flu vaccine, so I felt uncomfortable taking him out in public for 6 months. He didn't catch his first cold until he was close to one!" Although this mom seemed to be writing this with a great sense of pride, it was quite concerning to me. Her baby was not able to learn about all the interesting sights, smells, and sounds out there in the world and had little opportunity to socialize. And what about mom? As a psychologist, I am concerned that this mom might be prone to feelings of sadness, boredom, and isolation after staying in her home for 6 months!

When considering your comfort level with exposure to germs, be sure to weigh the costs and benefits. The benefit of limiting your child's exposure is that he is less likely to get the colds and stomach bugs that can crop up in the first year of life. The cost, however, might be that you (and even your baby) suffer. It is not selfish to admit that you are a mom who needs to be out and about to be happy. Remember that a happy mom is more likely to raise a happy baby. Dr. Weiser noted, "Babies should complement your life, not complicate it." If you enjoy getting out, doing things, and being around other people, feel free to continue doing this when baby arrives. If you really want to get back to work or need to get back to work, go ahead. Yes, your baby *will* pick up more germs than a baby who spends more time at home; however, babies are resilient. Furthermore, when they are exposed to germs they build up their immune systems. Eventually, you will have to face all the standard illnesses with your little one, whether he is 5 months old or 5 years old.

DEALING WITH ILLNESS INVOLVES A STEEP LEARNING CURVE. The first time your baby gets a cold or a fever it is terribly scary. Can you give her medicine? If so, what is the proper dose? How can you help her feel more comfortable? How many days should it be until she is well? New parents experience a great deal of uncertainty and intense feelings of responsibility when their children get sick. Negative thoughts tend to abound.

Calm Thinking helps a lot at a time like this. It is okay to not know what to do—that is why we have pediatricians! New moms aren't supposed to know how to practice medicine. If you are concerned about your baby, make an appointment as soon as possible. Keep in mind that anxiety can get in the way of processing and retaining information, so take a pen and paper with you. Write down the pediatrician's suggestions, and then read them back to ensure you understood them correctly. If you get home and something seems unclear, call back. The important thing is to remember that you are learning new skills. Each time your child falls ill, you will feel a greater sense of confidence in what to do to help her or him (and to help calm yourself).

DON'T BLAME YOURSELF. When illness or injury does happen, parents tend to blame themselves. Again, this is an important time to engage in Calm Thinking. Babies will get sick and they will get a bump and bruise here and there. These inevitable events are a part of childhood and do not equate to poor parenting.

At the same time, it can be helpful to be your own behavior therapist, particularly with respect to injuries. It is a good idea to baby-proof your home *before* your baby becomes mobile (e.g., putting gates at the top and bottom of the stairs, padding sharp corners on furniture, covering electrical outlets, putting locks on toilet lids). By doing so, you can prevent many accidents and focus on fine-tuning your baby-proofing as your baby begins to do things you would have never imagined (such as digging in potted plants, taking a bite out of yesterday's newspapers).

If an injury does occur, give some thought to whether this could be prevented in the future either by changing your behavior, changing the baby's behavior, or changing the environment. For example, consider an 8-month-old baby who pulled himself up on the coffee table, fell, and banged his chin on the sharp corner coming down. Even the most observant mom can't monitor a baby's every move or prevent every fall. A baby *should* be pulling himself up on furniture as he gets ready to walk. However, it is worth considering whether anything on the coffee table is particularly interesting to the baby. Indeed, in this situation our curious little guy was reaching for a plant. Mom could certainly deter her baby from pulling up on the coffee table by moving tempting objects off it. She could place his stuffed animals around the soft couches and chairs in the room to encourage him to pull up on those. She could further change the environment by putting protective covers on the corners of the coffee table or moving the coffee table out of the room for a while until her son is steadier on his feet.

To summarize, being a new parent involves an incredibly steep learning curve. Few jobs require the acquisition of as much new knowledge as quickly as being a parent. The final chapter of *Becoming a Calm Mom* can help you take stock of all you have accomplished by the end of your first year of motherhood. In the meantime, try to enjoy caring for your little one. Use your Calm Mom strategies and be open to trying several things until you find a solution that works for you and your baby. A word of warning: It often happens that after you solve one baby care dilemma, a new one pops up to present you with a whole new challenge. Don't be daunted by this. As you gain experience, you might find that discovering solutions to new challenges can actually seem like fun!

LOOKING AHEAD

For the first few months of being a new mom, most of your focus will be on your baby. As you feel calmer and more confident in your ability to care for your little one, you might find that you start focusing more on yourself. In chapter 5 I discuss all the challenges that you might be facing since you became a mother. I talk about solutions to these challenges again, drawing heavily from the Calm Mom Toolbox.

CHAPTER 5

REMAINING CALM WHEN "ME" BECOMES "MOM"

In this chapter, the focus is on moms. It is difficult to articulate the myriad reasons becoming a new mom can be so challenging. Perhaps one reason is that it affects everything—our thoughts and feelings about ourselves, our bodies, and our day-to-day activities. Another reason is that the effects can be quite subtle. New moms *know* they feel different than they did before becoming moms, but it is hard to describe what has changed. This can be disconcerting and makes it all the more challenging to come up with solutions to problems.

I have given this topic a great deal of thought through my own experiences, the experiences of my clients and friends, and the responses to the Calm Moms Survey. By putting it together I have broken down the challenges into four main categories: surprising emotions, loss of identity and freedom, loss of self-confidence, and loss of time for yourself. In this chapter I discuss each in turn, starting with an example, articulating the challenges, and then providing useful solutions that draw heavily from the Calm Mom strategies.

SURPRISING EMOTIONS

Before becoming moms, women assume that motherhood is going to be jam-packed with blissful moments. When reality, and the accompanying "less than blissful moments" set in, new moms are often taken aback. Consider the example of Lucy.

Example

Lucy could not wait for the day she would finally meet her baby boy. After a normal delivery, Peter was placed in her arms, and for the first hour or so Lucy felt just the way she had expected to feel: elated. She could not stop staring at tiny Peter, marveling that she and her husband had created such a beautiful creature. Then reality set in. Nursing was difficult and frustrating. She realized how exhausted and sore she felt from the delivery. She really just wanted someone else to whisk the baby away so she could get some rest.

The next couple of weeks followed a similar pattern of ups and downs. Some moments with Peter were simply heavenly. Yet there were many times Lucy had thoughts pop into her head that, frankly, took her by surprise: "I want a break," "I miss reading the paper and drinking coffee on Sunday mornings," and "I wonder what's going on at the office?" These thoughts led Lucy to much more painful thoughts: "I'm a terrible mother," "Why don't I feel more bonded?", and "It's so unfair that other people who really want kids can't have them—I have one and I want a break!"

The Challenges

The emotions associated with being a new mom are complex. We often hear new moms say that becoming a mother is the "best thing I ever did" or that they have "never been happier." We hear moms talk about how, when holding their baby for the first time, they felt that the whole world was suddenly right. The problem is that these emotional reactions are only part of the picture. When new moms experience any emotional reaction toward their baby or toward motherhood that is not glowingly positive, negative thoughts can begin. New moms can believe that something is wrong with them or that they don't deserve to be a mother because they have these thoughts.

The Solutions

What should new mothers do when faced with the myriad emotions they feel toward their babies and toward motherhood? Following are tips new mothers should keep in mind.

BONDING WITH YOUR BABY INVOLVES FORMING A NEW RELATIONSHIP—AND THIS CAN TAKE TIME. Some people assume that a woman will feel like a mother the minute her baby is placed in her arms. New moms believe they should *immediately* feel attached to the baby and *immediately* know what to do. For some women, this does happen. For many, it does not.

Let's take a step back from this assumption and do some Calm Thinking. Does this assumption make sense? It is helpful to think about bonding with respect to another significant person in your life, such as your spouse. How long did it take before you really bonded with and knew your spouse? Did you learn all his likes and dislikes on your first date? By the end of the first month you knew him, had you heard about all the early experiences that shaped who he is today? By the end of the first 6 months, did you know how to deal with all his moods or help him feel better when he was sick? It is quite possible that you are *still* getting to know your spouse and what makes him tick, even if you have known each other for years.

Bonding with a baby can take time as well. You are forming a relationship with another person, a person who is developing his

117

own personality and learning about the world around him. If you don't feel an immediate bond and immediate sense of confidence the moment your little one is placed in your arms, this does not mean you are a "bad" or "undeserving" mom. It probably means you are a normal mom. Check in with yourself each month. Do you feel more bonded with your baby this month than last? Do you feel more confident about your skills as a mom this month? Remind yourself that it is completely normal and appropriate to feel your love develop and grow with each passing month of your baby's life.

IT IS NORMAL (AND ACCEPTABLE) TO EXPERIENCE A WIDE RANGE OF EMOTIONS AS A NEW MOM. If a friend told you about a new job and said it was perfect in all respects, would you believe her? If a relative came back from a long-planned vacation and said there wasn't a thing he would have done differently, would you believe him? Most experiences in life encompass a range of emotion. A job may be interesting, offer opportunities for advancement, and pay well, but it may involve a long commute each day. A vacation may be in a fabulous location, with great food but may involve 7 straight days of rain. People have no qualms telling their friends about the positives and negatives of a new job or a recent vacation. Parenthood is totally different. New parents often feel they are supposed to rave about how wonderful every aspect of parenthood is, even if it is not true for them.

The problem with this expectation is that it is completely unreasonable. Although becoming a new mother offers innumerable moments of wonder, it also brings many moments that are not so positive. Dr. Donald Winnicott, a pediatrician and psychoanalyst born in England in 1896, summarized this issue perfectly in a 1960 radio address:

> There are some people who are rather shocked if they find they can have other than loving feelings toward small children . . .

We know well that every job has its frustrations and its boring routines and its times of being the last thing anyone would choose to do. Well, why shouldn't the care of babies and children be thought of that way too? (1993, pp. 65–67)

The question is how to deal with these "shocking" feelings. The tendency is to keep them to ourselves. Most people do not want to risk the negative judgments of others ("What kind of mother is she if she would like a morning to read the paper and drink coffee instead of being with her baby!"); furthermore, we do not want to admit these feelings to ourselves or admit that we are not perfectly performing the most important job we will ever have.

The key is to let your thoughts and feelings *be*. You don't need to do anything with them at all. Say to yourself, "I am feeling frustrated right now" and stop there. Do not allow yourself to progress to the next step, ". . . so I must be a terrible mom." You just had a *thought*—you didn't hit your child, deprive her of food, or leave her in a dirty diaper all day. At the end of a day, look back on your thoughts and feelings. If you felt frustrated when your little one would not stop crying, did you let this define your day? Or are you able to take a balanced look by recognizing that in any given day, every mom is going to have moments of joy and moments when she wants to scream or run off to a spa for a couple of weeks. That's life! The challenging moments make the special moments that much sweeter.

Honestly Share Your Experiences With Others. Dr. Winnicott had another useful suggestion for dealing with the emotional roller coaster that new moms find themselves on. He said, "I think mothers are *helped* by being able to voice their agonies at the time that they are experiencing them" (1993, p. 75; italics added for emphasis). Winnicott implies that women who are least afraid to "look at their other feelings" are "women who do love their children" (p. 75). Sounds a lot like the Calm Companionship strategy, doesn't it?

As I discuss in chapter 7, new moms can benefit from seeking out new friends who are in the thick of new motherhood. As you establish these friendships, be honest about your experiences. When you are honest about the good, the bad, and the ugly of new motherhood, you encourage your friends to do the same. Within an honest friendship a few great things happen. First, you learn you are not alone. This makes women feel more confident about their skills as moms and lets them feel supported by people who really know what it is like. Second, you learn valuable lessons. A fellow new mother might offer a great solution to a problem, a solution you may not have thought about on your own.

LOSS OF IDENTITY AND FREEDOM

Prior to having children, women tend to lead independent lives. Each day involves choices. Do I want to work late tonight or go to the gym? Do I want to cook dinner for me and my spouse or pop out to a restaurant? When children arrive, we lose the freedom to make these seemingly simple choices. We can also start feeling that we've lost our sense of who we are. Consider the example of Mallory.

Example

Mallory accomplished a lot before she got married when she was 35 years old. She worked as a journalist, traveling all over the world to cover current events. Mallory spent most of her time working, but on her days off she enjoyed hiking, sailing, and seeing movies with friends. She kept a frenetic schedule and lived life to its fullest. At age 33, she met her husband; at 35, they tied the knot. Mallory's life did not change much when she got married. She continued to travel a great deal and when she was home, she and her husband kept a busy social life.

Six months after they married, Mallory got pregnant. As she had complications early in her pregnancy, her obstetrician recommended cutting back on travel. When she spoke to her newspaper editor about restricting travel, he reassigned her to what Mallory described as a "mundane desk job." After wrenching conversations with her husband, she decided to stop working at the newspaper. She knew she wanted to stay home with the baby for at least a year, so it made sense to call it quits now and follow her doctor's advice to take it easy.

Mallory enjoyed her time away from work during pregnancy. She did a lot of things in her own city that she usually did not have time to do. She spent a lot of time with friends and family, got ready for the baby, and read lots of books. She also enjoyed her first few months of motherhood. But at the 3-month mark, Mallory started to feel pretty low.

Mallory started to miss her old life. When she read the newspaper each day she missed being part of the action. She missed talking to people about her exciting travels, her opinions on world affairs, or her latest sailing adventure. She began to feel resentful about people asking her about her baby, as she felt they were forgetting that she was her own person. As the realities of new motherhood set in, Mallory recognized that she did not have the freedom to just run out for dinner with friends, let alone spend a whole day sailing. Although she greatly enjoyed her new baby and found it exciting to watch him grow and develop, she definitely felt that too much of the old Mallory had gone missing.

The Challenges

As Mallory found, the first month or so after having a baby can feel surreal. New moms often say that they cannot quite believe that the baby is theirs . . . to keep . . . . forever. It almost seems as though life could go back to normal at any moment, like waking from a dream.

Then reality sets in. New moms realize that a little person has moved into their home and isn't going anywhere for about 18 years! As reality hits, parents realize their lives have changed forever, in every possible way. Yes, life has changed in innumerable wonderful ways. But what about the less wonderful stuff? New moms often talk about "losses" after they have "gained" a baby. These losses can contribute to some of the negative emotions that moms experience.

Mallory's story highlights two significant losses for new moms: loss of identity and loss of freedom. Loss of identity can mean many different things. Moms who stop working when they have a baby often feel they have lost an important part of their identity. When Mallory stopped working as a journalist, she no longer felt like a journalist and people no longer considered her one. This became most salient to Mallory when people no longer asked her opinion on important current events or asked to hear stories about her latest travels to the front lines of the news.

Our identities can also be tied up in our leisure activities. Before having a baby, Mallory traveled, hiked, and sailed. All these defining parts of her seemingly vanished when she had a baby, only to be replaced by endless feedings, diaper changes, and playgroups.

Our identities can also be tied to other people—we are wives, daughters, and friends. When all our time and attention is captured by a baby, we might feel we have lost the important roles we play in other people's lives.

As if it were not difficult enough to see ourselves differently when we become moms, our conversations with others serve to confirm all those changes. Suddenly it seems every conversation opens with: "How's the baby?" or "What's the baby doing?" Suddenly new moms wonder if anyone cares about them or their interests and talents separate from being a mom.

Some new moms also experience a loss of freedom. This can affect virtually every aspect of your life. In the first couple of days at home with a new baby, you realize you cannot even go to the bathroom on your own schedule anymore. You quickly learn to make a bathroom stop *before* beginning to feed the baby. And don't new babies have an uncanny habit of becoming voraciously hungry just as mommy sits down to eat? From the day before you give birth to the day you give birth, new moms experience a major shift from "me first" to "baby first."

Loss of freedom influences more significant areas of life too. When you have a child you cannot decide to work late, meet friends for dinner, or go for an early morning jog on a whim. It seems that every decision takes major planning. Even the best-laid plans, such as a special dinner out with your spouse, can come crashing down when baby comes down with a fever or a babysitter cancels.

The Solutions

Solving the problems of loss of identity and freedom are far from easy. When women have babies, their lives change in every way possible. How can we become more comfortable with these changes?

ACCEPT THAT BECOMING A NEW MOM IS A MAJOR ROLE ADJUSTMENT AND GIVE IT SOME TIME. Expecting to feel comfortable with the new role of "mom" the moment the little one is placed in your arms is completely unrealistic. There is no book, class, or babysitting experience in the world that can prepare you for what this amazing experience is *really* like. It can be extremely helpful if moms give themselves permission to feel uncomfortable while they adjust to this significant new role.

Many new moms commented on how long it took them to really feel like a mother in the context of the Calm Moms Survey question, "How has having a baby affected your identity?" Here are three typical responses:

- "The new addition to our lives took about 3 months to really get comfortable and let it all sink in."
- "Things came together for me around 7 months to a year after the baby was born."
- "I would say that I adjusted to the new role of 'mom' by my son's first birthday."

These responses suggest that taking on a new role is a process, and a slowly unfolding one at that. As our babies change and grow, so do we. We learn every day about the skills involved in being a mom, our general approach to parenting, ways to navigate our marital relationship when baby makes three, ways to balance career and home, ways to maintain interests and hobbies while accepting that some must be temporarily put on hold, and so on. Our personalities grow and change as well when we become new moms. Few, if any, of these changes can happen overnight; expecting that they should will undoubtedly lead to a great sense of disappointment and frustration.

FOCUS ON GAINS INSTEAD OF LOSSES. Women who are expecting their first baby often express the fear of losing their identity after they become moms. Ruminating about these issues before you have had a baby is probably futile. It is impossible to know how changes in your identity will affect you until your life as a mother begins.

Many women who responded to the Calm Moms Survey question about identity focused on the *positive* changes they had undergone since they became a mother. Here are some of the responses:

- "I think motherhood has enhanced my identity. I'm more social now than ever because I have met many interesting moms and we are going to play dates, etc."
- "I actually feel much wiser and more accomplished after having my baby. I think having kids is the toughest job in the world and knowing that I can handle it makes me feel good about myself."
- "Mostly I feel that I have gained a new dimension. I have lost time for part of my pre-mom self, but it's still there—just not as much a priority."

The most obvious change is gaining the new role of mom. Yes, it is daunting, tiring, and all consuming. But it is also quite amazing. Many new moms talk about acquiring a sense of patience they never knew they had. Many talk about impressing themselves with their ability to balance many different roles and responsibilities. Many love sharing knowledge, passions, and interests with their little ones. New moms often feel a sense of pride in teaching their children good manners and values or introducing them at an early age to special interests such as religion, the arts, or a love of nature. In effect, acquiring the identity of "mom" involves helping to shape the identity of another human being. I can't think of two better words for describing that experience than the ones mentioned at the beginning of this paragraph—daunting, yet amazing!

Many new moms also find that their identities in other areas grow and change when they become moms. For example, many women chart new career paths they never could have imagined prior to becoming moms. I never imagined I would be writing a book about new moms instead of about anxiety disorders! I met many women whose career paths changed as they acquired the role of *mom,* including a woman who started a company that offers fitness classes and personal training to new moms, a mom who launched a

Web site that lists resources for new moms in our area, and a mom who started a business selling nursing supplies. There are wonderful success stories out there about "mom entrepreneurs" who became hugely successful by starting businesses that mattered to new moms and that were achievable when staying home with kids.

New moms often acquire new leisure pursuits as a result of having babies. Some who take prenatal yoga classes become lifelong yoga aficionados. Others become motivated to work on charitable pursuits that suddenly touch close to home when they have children of their own.

Another way our identities grow and change when we become new moms is through the people we meet. Having a new baby often means meeting other people with new babies, be it in a breast-feeding support group, at a baby music class, or in line at the grocery store. You might find yourself becoming friends with people with whom you have worked with for years but barely known, simply because you now have the common bond of children. New friendships often introduce us to new interests and new ways of looking at the world. These little sparks can in turn redefine who we are.

DO WHAT YOU NEED TO DO TO BRING BACK THE IMPORTANT PARTS OF YOUR PREBABY IDENTITY. This might be perceived as a case of exuberant optimism. There is no doubt that along with the positive growth and change associated with becoming a new mom, there are also losses that can lead to anxiety and unhappiness. The example of Mallory highlights this problem. In the months surrounding the birth of her baby, her life practically stopped in its tracks. Suddenly, all the activities and interests that had defined her for years were no longer a part of her life, and she felt empty.

This is a time to be your own behavior therapist. Think back to your prebaby life. What brought you a feeling of mastery—a feeling that you were good at something or accomplishing something important? What brought you a sense of pleasure? How did you have fun? Think about what behavioral changes you need to make in your current life to bring these feelings back.

When Mallory reflected on these questions she came to some interesting conclusions. She realized she did not really miss leisure pursuits such as hiking and sailing. She figured she would get back into these activities soon enough, with husband and baby in tow. What she did miss was work. She recognized that she gained a sense of both mastery and pleasure from working. She felt good about breaking news stories with the public and felt she really was good at it. She also had fun doing it. After much discussion with her husband, she set up an appointment to speak to her former boss. She explained that she didn't want a boring desk job but also didn't want to travel or be separated from her baby. Fortuitously, a reporter who covered local human-interest stories had just left the paper. This was an area Mallory never thought to cover in the past when she was jetting off to write about natural disasters and wars. Yet she sensed that at this time in her life, it might just fit the bill.

An important tip should be highlighted as part of this discussion: **Decisions are rarely permanent.** New moms often feel stuck. We beat ourselves up for making a mistake or worry that people will judge us badly for going back on seemingly sensible decisions. Remember that over time, it is normal and appropriate to make all sorts of adjustments in our lives so we feel well rounded and satisfied.

Another important tip is that it is not selfish to continue to do things you enjoyed before having children. As noted earlier, happier moms make for happier babies. You might not be able to do it all, but it can help to make a list of things that you miss, rank them in terms of importance, and try to bring at least the top one or two back into your life. Doing so will take some creativity and flexibility. Did you love to exercise? Then try to find an exercise class in your area that includes babies. Did you love seeing movies? See if there is a theatre in your area that shows afternoon movies at which babies are welcome. My husband is a huge Washington Redskins football fan and had season's tickets for years, even though we live in Philadelphia. It is no longer practical for us to spend an entire day driving to Washington, DC (we live 3 hours away!), enjoying the game, and driving all the way home. We now enjoy games in our living room. My husband gets our little girl all decked out in Redskins regalia, they play and watch the game, and I make a fun dinner. It's not the same as being there, but my husband has been able to maintain this part of his identity after becoming a dad. He knows that in a few years, he will again be making the trek to Washington, DC, and will be able to share all the excitement with his children.

Parents should also remember that it is fine to have a family member or trusted babysitter watch the baby so they can continue to do the things they enjoy that are not practical with a baby in tow. When I first became a mom, I frequently missed my monthly book club because it kept falling on nights that my husband had to work. When I really thought about what I was missing since becoming a mom, this was it—chatting about books and sharing a relaxing meal with my group of girlfriends. Now the day after our next book club meeting is planned, I find out whether my husband has to work; if he does, I arrange for a babysitter. I expected to feel guilty the first time I did this, but I didn't. I was able to put my daughter to bed before I left so it had no affect on her at all, and I got to enjoy doing something that was an important part of my premom identity.

LOSS OF SELF-CONFIDENCE

All of the challenges associated with having a new baby can change even the most self-confident woman into a quivering bundle of nerves. Consider the example of Pamela.

Example

Pamela had always been a self-assured woman. She did well at her job as manager of a popular clothing store. She was also artistic and sold her paintings in local art shows. She had married her high school sweetheart, Phil, when they were just 20 years old. Although people told her she was marrying too young, their marriage was still going strong 7 years later when they decided to have a baby. Pamela decided that she would take 3 months off when the baby arrived and could not wait to meet the little bundle of joy.

When Pamela's baby was born, she was completely committed to nursing. But things just were not working out. Various difficulties with nursing caused her baby to not gain sufficient weight; the pediatrician told her she must supplement with formula. Pamela felt like a complete failure. Things got worse from there. Pamela, previously an incredibly energetic woman, felt as though she was getting nothing done in a day. She made lists of things to do, as she always had, but by the end of the day crossed nothing off the list. She couldn't figure out what she was doing all day. She started to view herself as lazy and unmotivated. To make matters worse, Pamela constantly compared herself with her friends who were also new moms. She looked at them and saw them as more committed to their babies (because they were nursing) and more efficient (because they seemed to be getting more done each day than she was). They even seemed to have lost their baby weight faster than she. Pamela could not see a single thing in her life that she was doing right.

The Challenges

Motherhood has a way of plunging even the most self-assured women into a pool of self-doubt. People assume that because being a mother is the "most natural job in the world" they will immediately feel comfortable with it and do everything perfectly. How is it possible to have trouble nursing? How can it be that a mom might have difficulties soothing her baby? Is it possible that a new mom might not know how to play with a baby?

The example of Pamela demonstrates two things. First, motherhood can come with a lot of social comparisons—evaluating whether we measure up to other moms, or sometimes to our own moms. Too often, we decide that we fall short. The job of motherhood also comes with a lot of "should's"—things we feel we *should* be good at, feelings we think we *should* have. Albert Ellis, a famous psychologist, developed Rational Emotive Behavior Therapy, a kind of cognitive behavior therapy. He did research on the negative thoughts held by his therapy clients and found that a majority fell into the category of "an unconditional, ought or must" (1998, p. 38). Ellis, a man with a unique sense of humor, labeled this kind of thinking, *musterbation.* He wrote that "musts directed against the self" were "a very common form of musterbation which people all over the world often have at many points in their lives, lead[ing] them to feel anxious, depressed, worthless, self-hating, and insecure when they do not achieve various goals in their lives" (p. 39). Have you been *musterbating* since becoming a mom?

The Solutions

The biggest problem with comparing ourselves with others and holding ourselves up to excessively high standards is that we set ourselves up for failure. We become so focused on all the ways that we are not measuring up that we fail to focus on all the wonderful things associated with being a new mom. Luckily, there are simple ways to stop musterbating and stop comparing ourselves with others. Give some thought to these solutions.

SET REASONABLE STANDARDS FOR YOURSELF. I have a bold suggestion for new moms in their first month or two of motherhood. Simplify your notion of what you can accomplish in a day. I suggest three simple goals a day.

First, take care of your baby. This means feeding him, keeping him clean, helping him to rest, playing with him during his periods of alertness, and showing him warmth and affection. There are a few important things to notice. First, there are no qualifiers. You have not failed if you feed your baby with formula instead of breast milk. You have not failed if you pick your little one up from his play mat and realize that there has been a diaper malfunction (as long as you remedy the situation!). You have not failed if you do not know the words to every nursery rhyme and children's song. You have not failed if your baby spends most of a day fussing and crying. Succeeding at this goal simply means ensuring that your baby is healthy and loved each day.

Second, take care of yourself. By this I mean get some sleep, take a shower each day, and eat healthfully. As you will read in greater detail later in this chapter, doing these things is the opposite of selfish—they are essential to succeeding at this amazingly hard job of motherhood.

Third, set *one* non-baby-related goal. ONE. This means making one phone call, writing one thank you note, tidying up one room in your house, doing one load of laundry. Remember our discussion earlier in this book about feeding babies? The daily hours spent feeding your baby is equivalent to the hours you used to spend at your full-time job. Well, as there are other essentials involved in daily baby care, this means there is very little time for anything else. Your priorities should be caring for the baby and yourself. After that you can worry about cleaning the bathroom. When you set the goal of doing one non-baby-related task a day, an amazing thing happens—most of the time you succeed. Give yourself a pat on the back even if accomplishing the task might have seemed like the easiest thing just a few short months ago.

After you get a better handle on being a mom and your baby is less labor intensive (eating every three hours instead of every two!), you might widen your goals . . . a bit. Trust me, it will be quite a few *years* before you can accomplish in a day what you used to before you had a baby. Remember to set reasonable goals, give yourself a pat on the back for a job well done, and cut yourself some slack if other things get in the way of completing everything you had mapped out for one day.

DON'T COMPARE YOURSELF WITH OTHERS. The problem with social comparisons is that they can be fraught with bias (and even when they are not, they just aren't helpful). Many new moms get caught up with what other mothers *say* they are feeling or doing: "Jenny says she is feeling totally comfortable with being a new mom and her baby is only 1 week old" or "Evelyn says she is back to running three miles a day even though her baby is only 6 weeks old." Remember—new moms do not want to admit weakness! When new mothers only talk about how great everything is, it might be that they are ashamed to share the aspects of motherhood that are going less well. Take what they say with a grain of salt. Try to set up in your friendships an environment in which it is okay to share *all* aspects of motherhood, not just the ones that are going well. This will make your friendships better for you and for your friends.

Another thing to consider is whether your own negative feelings affect the impressions you have of others. Don't selectively pay attention to things that suggest other moms are managing better than you are while ignoring things that suggest other new moms are struggling. After spending an afternoon with Evelyn you might come home thinking only about her athletic prowess, rather than the fact she told you that she often cries when her baby is crying because she just doesn't know how to soothe her. This is not to imply that you should focus on others' frailties but to suggest that you ask if you are considering the whole picture or only the part that supports a negative view of yourself.

Discussing motherhood with our own mothers can be problematic too. Some make it seem as though motherhood was much harder in the days before you could plunk your baby in front of *Sesame Street* or amuse her with a never-ending rotation of educational toys. This leaves us thinking, "Gee, I can't handle this even with TV and a million toys—what's wrong with me?" Some of our mothers seem to recall their own early motherhood in only the most glowing terms. The only thing I ever heard my mother complain about with respect to raising babies was that my sister projectile vomited for the first year of her life, necessitating frequent cleaning of every wall in the house. Otherwise, her memory of new motherhood seemed to be quite positive. It was only after she gave me her journal that recounted her experiences during my first year of life that I realized she encountered many of the same challenges I had. With the passage of time, however, memories of the day-to-day challenges had disappeared.

Putting all this together, there is one conclusion: Comparing yourself with others often brings you one thing—bad feelings about yourself. Try to stop comparisons. Just don't make them! They are not helpful. Rather, accept whatever you are thinking or feeling without reference to others. Have you had a difficult day? That's fine. It doesn't matter if your friend seems to have never had one in her life! Did you feel frustrated by your baby today? Okay. It doesn't matter if your mom claims she never found you frustrating (until you were in high school).

At the end of a day, try to come to an unbiased view of what you have experienced. Was the entire day difficult and frustrating?

Or were there some precious moments in there too? Taking a few minutes at the end of the day to reflect can be helpful in showing you that few days are overarchingly bad. It is just that we new moms beat ourselves up so much about the challenges that we forget to pat ourselves on the back for the successes.

LOSS OF TIME FOR YOURSELF

Before having children, out time is our own. Barring time spent at work, the rest of our hours are spent according to what we want to do. When baby arrives, this changes drastically. Carving any time out for ourselves becomes a challenge. Consider the example of Gillian.

Example

About a month into new motherhood Gillian started to feel low. She felt as though her days were a blur of feedings with a bit of fun play time in between. When her son slept she rushed around the house throwing in loads of laundry, cooking meals, and checking e-mails from her job, despite being on maternity leave. She was completely exhausted but could not figure out when it would be possible to sneak in a nap.

Although before having her baby she worried about how she would ever lose her pregnancy weight, Gillian now realized that those concerns were unfounded. As she rarely found time to eat the pounds seemed to be disappearing by the day. Although her physique was in better shape than she had expected, she felt like a total mess. She did not shower until the evening, after her husband came home from work. She was living in sweatpants and hadn't so much as opened her cosmetics case since the day before giving birth. One day, Gillian called her mother in tears. When her mom asked what was wrong, Gillian said, "I know this sounds so selfish, but there is no time for *me* anymore."

The Challenges

The first few weeks of being a new mom are often a total blur of feeding, diaper changes, and astonishingly loud and frequent crying! Our focus is almost exclusively on our little ones—and for the most part, that feels fine. However, as the weeks tick by this singular focus can take a toll. It is ironic that when our bodies are trying to recover from pregnancy and childbirth, we feel so unable to attend to our own needs. And during this major period of role adjustment, it is difficult to know how much time and attention we *should* be giving to ourselves. A new mom can feel that doing anything for herself is selfish. As you will read in the following section, this kind of thinking is just flat-out wrong!

The Solutions

A discussion of good eating and exercise habits for new moms is provided at the end of this chapter (the importance of sleep is noted in chap. 4). However, before addressing those needs, there are three important solutions to the challenge of not having any time for yourself after a baby joins your family.

LOOKING AFTER YOURSELF IS NOT SELFISH. The most important tip to keep in mind is that it is not even remotely selfish to look after yourself while you are also looking after your baby. A mom who hasn't showered by 2:00 p.m., who hasn't eaten a square meal in days, and who hasn't done anything for herself in weeks is going to be one thing and one thing only: an unhappy mom. Babies can sense tension and unhappiness, so it is important that you are nurtured too. It is essential for your physical and emotional well-being and will make it much easier for you to nurture your baby, too. Your baby will be happier and calmer because of it!

DON'T IGNORE PROBLEMS. New moms are often so focused on their babies that they ignore their own needs. This is not a good idea, because all sorts of problems can crop up in the postpartum period. Just as you check your baby to make sure he is comfortable, well fed, and clean, check in with yourself. Set a time once a day to do this.

First, check your mood. I discuss postpartum depression and anxiety in greater detail in the appendix. The importance of monitoring your mood and ensuring that as the weeks pass, you gradually begin to feel calmer and more confident in your new role as mom, cannot be underestimated. If you feel extremely sad and tearful, or extremely nervous and anxious, seek help from a mental health professional (your obstetrician should be able to help you with referrals).

Next, make sure you are healing well after having your baby. If you have any concerns, call your obstetrician or book an appointment. There is no reason to wait until the standard 6-week postpartum checkup if you have a concern.

Finally, make sure you are meeting your basic needs on a daily basis. Are you eating healthfully, drinking plenty of fluids (particularly important if you are nursing), getting some sleep, getting some fresh air and exercise, and practicing basic hygiene? If you identify a problem, consider ways to remedy it as soon as possible. Your baby is depending on having a healthy mom!

HAVE REASONABLE EXPECTATIONS. Keep in mind that you were pregnant for 9 months (that's just 3 months short of a year). Your body went through vast changes. Although we have all heard about women who leave the hospital in size 2 jeans and start running 5 miles a day a week after giving birth, these women are rarities or simply the stuff of folk legend. Your body is going to take time to feel normal again. It might take a few months to lose that baby weight. It might take even longer to feel as though you had an adequate night's sleep. When women breast-feed it can take longer for the body to look and feel as it did before becoming pregnant. There is nothing wrong with working toward goals—such as losing baby weight—but be sure your goals are reasonable. Consulting with your obstetrician on such matters can be helpful.

With these three general tips established, let's consider the important issues of weight, eating, body image, and exercise.

WEIGHT, EATING, AND BODY IMAGE

It is recommended that women gain 25 to 35 pounds during pregnancy—slightly more if they were underweight when they became pregnant and slightly less if they were overweight when they became pregnant. Giving birth gets rid of some of this weight—the baby accounts for about 7.5 pounds and the amniotic fluid, placenta, extra fluids floating around in your body (remember those swollen ankles?), and an enlarged uterus and breasts account for another 12 to 20 pounds. But it is unrealistic to expect that when you leave the hospital you will have achieved your prepregnancy weight or that you will look like your prepregnancy self. You won't.

So what's a new mom to do? I have mentioned it already, but I will say it again—**have reasonable expectations.** It took 9 months to put on the weight and for your body to change in such significant ways—it might take 9 months or more to get back to normal. So if you are standing in front of the mirror 1 week after giving birth and are engaging in a critique of your pouch-like stomach and saggy breasts, do some Calm Thinking. Remind yourself, "It is unrealistic to expect to look like my 'old self' right now." Rather than beating yourself up, start thinking about the realistic steps you *can* take to accomplish your goals.

Don't Engage in Restrictive Eating

For a number of reasons, restrictive eating (or *crash dieting*) is not a good idea for new moms (or anyone else, for that matter). First, research has shown that food deprivation backfires and often results in overeating. As soon as you severely restrict your calories or forbid yourself certain foods, you are putting yourself at risk for eating more than if you had eaten a healthy, well-rounded diet. Second, this same body of research shows that food deprivation is associated with low mood and feelings of anxiety. New moms are already prone to low mood and feelings of anxiety because of hormonal changes they are experiencing as well as the challenges associated with caring for a newborn. It is unwise to exacerbate these feelings by severely restricting your eating. Third, nutritious food is important for a body that is healing. Childbirth is no easy feat, and your body needs fuel to recover, particularly if you had a caesarean section or a particularly difficult vaginal birth. Finally, nutritious food is essential for breast-feeding. A food- and fluid-deprived mother cannot produce enough milk to properly nurture a baby.

Feed Yourself, Not Just Your Baby

Hopefully, after reading the last paragraph you will be convinced to drop your plan to eat only an apple each day until you reach your prebaby weight! What should you eat instead? It is a good idea to **eat three meals and a snack or two each day.** Spacing meals and snacks throughout the day ensures a steady stream of energy, which all new moms need. Be sure to keep well hydrated, particularly if you are nursing. **Allow yourself to eat a range of foods.** This means avoiding the trap of *forbidden foods,* foods that you do not permit yourself to have. As already noted above, having a list of forbidden foods increases the likelihood of binging on those foods when you do have access to them. Treats are fine as long as they are consumed in moderation and as part of a diet that consists of lots of fruits, vegetables, whole grains, and healthy proteins. There is nothing wrong with having a square of delicious chocolate after a lunch of a big salad with a grilled chicken breast. Keep in mind that eating healthfully definitely takes some planning. Before setting out for the grocery store, make a list of things you would like to have in the house to accomplish your eating goals. Buy healthy foods in as convenient a form as possible. For example, buy bagged salads and frozen, precooked chicken breasts if you think you would enjoy a chicken salad for lunch. Have your husband or your mother whip you up a big pot of pasta with fresh vegetables and put it away in portion-sized plastic containers in the fridge. There is no doubt that as a new mother your free time is limited, so being organized will help you accomplish your weight-loss goals. Finally, **allow yourself the time to eat.** Being home with a new baby can take on a frenzied pace. It often feels as though there isn't time to eat or that eating is selfish, particularly when the baby needs something. Eating is time well spent. It will give you the energy and patience that you need to be a calm new mom.

Stop Bad Pregnancy Habits

For some women, pregnancy is a license to eat anything and everything under the sun! After baby arrives, it is important to get back to good habits. This includes **being aware of portion size.** If you were eating two cups of cooked pasta for lunch when you were pregnant, cut back to one cup. A lot of nutrition experts suggest eating off smaller plates. This is a reasonable way to ensure that you do not overeat—and much simpler than counting calories. Getting back to good habits also means **cutting back on the splurges** that pregnant women allow themselves, such as fast food or nightly bowls of ice cream. Although a moderate serving of French fries or ice cream is fine, caloric and fatty foods should be consumed only occasionally, balanced out by more frequent encounters with baked potatoes or low-fat frozen yogurt!

Exercise

Bookstores are filled with books promising the latest "get skinny quick" scheme. When faced with losing 40 pregnancy pounds, new moms are liable to try anything. Let me save you some money! There is a very simple equation: **calories in + energy out = pounds lost or gained.** The only reliable way to lose weight is to consume fewer calories and to exercise more. Exercise has many other benefits beyond weight loss. It improves mood, provides a boost of energy, and is a great way to spend time with other moms. Check out postnatal exercise classes in your area (see "Resources for New Moms" at the end of this book for suggestions). These classes are designed to be done with baby in tow, so you can't use your little one as an excuse for not getting fit!

Consider Your Clothes

Before you skip over this paragraph, slow down and read! I promise that this is not a silly tip! One source of body image difficulties for new moms is the mistaken belief that they will come out of the hospital able to wear their prepregnancy clothes. If you go home and try to squeeze into your size 6 jeans one day after giving birth, you will gain two things—bruised thighs and a bruised ego! Be prepared to spend more time in maternity clothes, probably the ones you wore early in your pregnancy. Then as the weight comes off, you might need to go out and buy a few new items of clothing. It takes time to get back to your old size, and some women notice that their old clothes never fit properly again after all the physical changes that happened during pregnancy. As a nursing mom, I found that many of my prepregnancy shirts did not fit again until I finished nursing. There is nothing worse for a woman's body image than to wear clothes that don't fit or to repeatedly try to get into clothes that might never fit again (even if you do take off all the weight). Go out and treat yourself. You don't need to buy anything fancy because your clothes will take a beating from the frequent spit-ups and the other stuff that new babies produce. Simply make sure your new clothes are comfortable, washable, and help you feel attractive, regardless of the size on the tag.

Be Your Own Behavior Therapist

The basic way to lose that baby weight is to have reasonable expectations; give yourself permission to eat regular, well-balanced, healthy meals with the occasional small treat; and get out there and exercise. Easier said than done, right? Acting as your own behavior therapist can help you accomplish your eating and exercise goals. Let's consider the example of Shelly.

Shelly was motivated to take off her baby weight. For the most part she was doing well, particularly with respect to getting rid of bad pregnancy habits such as eating too many fried foods (which had made her feel better during her first trimester). However, she just could not shed the final ten pounds that she wanted to lose. Shelly got frustrated one day and reflected on what she was doing wrong. She identified two problems: eating a snack after the baby's 10:00 p.m. feeding each night and lack of exercise. She gave further thought to the factors maintaining these problematic behaviors. Her husband had to go to work early in the morning, so he usually went to sleep by 10:00 p.m. Shelly found that after she fed the baby at that hour she needed a bit of relaxation, and she often found herself in the kitchen preparing a bowl of ice cream to eat in front of the TV. She considered what else she might be able to do to relax. She decided it was important that she stay away from the kitchen, because as soon as she went into that room she wanted ice cream! She also figured out that she associated nighttime talk shows with eating ice cream. Before having a baby Shelly enjoyed reading, but she felt too mentally exhausted in those first few postpartum months to really follow a book. She wondered whether now, in her fifth month of motherhood, she might be able to get back into reading, as she was more well rested than she had been at the beginning. The next day Shelly went to the bookstore with the baby and picked out some light novels. That night after the 10:00 p.m. feeding she found a quiet place far from the kitchen and the TV to read. She read for ten minutes, got drowsy, and went to bed. She continued this routine for a week or so. Shelly noticed a number of advantages of her new routine. She cut down her ice cream consumption, was getting a lot of pleasure out of reading, and was actually getting more sleep as reading helped her unwind more quickly than TV had.

Shelly also thought about why she was not exercising. Prior to having a baby she used to walk every night after dinner with her husband. Now when her husband got home from work he wanted to spend time with the baby; he felt that pushing the baby in a stroller wasn't quite the same as getting down on the floor and playing. Shelly came to realize that she liked the social nature of exercise— she enjoyed chatting with her husband as they walked. Shelly called a friend who also had a baby and they made plans to walk three times a week with their babies. This plan worked well for Shelly. Adding exercise to her week did help her to gradually take off the last bit of baby weight and provided a nice social interaction.

LOOKING AHEAD

You may notice that in discussing new moms in this chapter, I glossed over a very important issue: whether or not to work outside the home after you become a new mom. Rest assured that I have not forgotten this topic. Chapter 6 is dedicated to this complex decision. Read on to learn more about the unique challenges facing both stay-at-home moms and moms who work outside the home. I hope you find the suggested solutions helpful, regardless of which path you choose to take.

CHAPTER 6

TO WORK OR NOT TO WORK, THAT IS THE QUESTION

Chapter 5 was all about moms. You might, however, have noticed a lack of attention to a major issue facing new moms—whether or not to work outside the home. This issue is so complex that I believe it warrants its own chapter. As in previous chapters, the Facts about women and work are presented. Then I discuss the Challenges facing both working and stay-at-home moms. Finally, helpful Solutions are offered for the unique challenges facing these two groups.

BEING A WORKING MOM

The Facts

According to a United States Census Bureau survey released in 2002, 72% of women who do not have children are in the labor force. In contrast, only 55% of mothers with infants under the age of one are in the labor force. Mothers of infants are more likely to work if they have college degrees (63%) and if they are 30 years old or older (61%). Interestingly, 72% of mothers with children over age one are in the labor force, suggesting that women return to work soon after having a child.

There do not appear to be formal scientific studies on the reasons women return to the workforce after having children, but there are two likely determinants. The first is financial. The American Academy of Pediatrics (2004) explains that for many families, particularly single-parent families, "the alternative to a working mother is poverty." Even in two-parent homes, few families can afford to live on one salary. This compels many new mothers to return to work. The second reason many women return to work is that their work is an important part of their identities. Some women feel that they have simply put in too many years of education and training to give up their work. Other women enjoy working and, despite being excited about becoming moms, cannot imagine a life without work.

New moms are faced with two important questions when considering whether to return to work. (a) Will I be more stressed out as a working mom than as a stay-at-home mom? (b) Is there any evidence to suggest that kids turn out better when raised exclusively by parents rather than with the regular involvement of other people (such as a nanny or commercial day care providers)? The complete answers to both these complex questions are beyond the scope of this book; however, we can consider each briefly.

There is no clear answer to the first question. Working outside the home is associated with both positive and negative effects. As compared with stay-at-home moms, those who work outside the home tend to have higher self-esteem, better mental health (less anxiety and depression), and not surprisingly, higher social status and better financial resources. However, being a working mom has also been found to be associated with greater levels of stress than being a stay-at-home mom. Possible contributing factors to this increased stress include role overload (the feeling of excessive demands at *both* work and home; Ross & Mirowsky, 1992), high levels of work–family spillover caused by the spouse's job (e.g., when the spouse's job is so demanding that it interferes in family life and leaves mom responsible for most aspects of family life), and dissatisfaction with child care arrangements (see Tingey, Kiger, & Riley, 1996). The presence of these factors has been found to essentially cancel out the positive effects associated with working. However, for women who do not report experiencing these stressors, working seems to have a generally positive impact on well-being.

In response to our second question, about the effects of child care on children, we are fortunate to be able to draw from an excellent research study called the National Institute of Child Health and Human Development (NICHD) Study of Early Child Care and Youth Development. The NICHD study is the most comprehensive study done as yet to examine the impact of early child care on later development. This longitudinal study has followed 1,000 babies since they were born in 1991. The children who are participating in the study live throughout the country and come from a wide range of socioeconomic backgrounds. The study has yielded over 60 published research studies, but here are a few select findings of interest to new moms.

First, the amount of time a child spends in child care each week is associated with increased school readiness, better language development, greater social competence, and better peer interaction skills. As noted later in chapter 6, most moms who responded to the Calm Moms Survey whose babies were in child care discussed these advantages. The carefully conducted NICHD study provides strong research support for these casual observations.

The second finding that deserves mention is that the amount of time a child spends in child care each week is also associated with increased behavior problems. This finding has been reported frequently by the media, causing panic among moms all over the country. However, it is essential to note that the NICHD study found that these behavior problems were still within the normal range. Being in child care is not turning kids into super-aggressive, nasty little demons. Rather, children in child care tend to score at the higher end of the normal range for behavior problems, whereas children who stay home with their moms tend to score at the lower end of the normal range for behavior problems.

Finally, the NICHD study found that quality of parenting has stronger effects on child outcomes than any aspect of the child care experience. In other words, even if children are raised by working parents and thus spend less time in the company of their parents, what parents do with their children in the home is the single greatest predictor of how their kids turn out.

With these facts established, let's turn our attention to the challenges associated with being a working mom. Later in this chapter I discuss the challenges associated with being a stay-at-home mom. Helpful solutions will be presented for both groups of women.

The Challenges

There are countless reasons returning to work can be so challenging for new moms. Perhaps the most challenging is **child care arrangements**. The choices are difficult for so many reasons beyond the most obvious one—entrusting one's newborn infant to the care of someone besides you. Because maternity leave tends to be so brief in the United States, parents often have to make decisions about child care before they have even had their babies. Sometimes a decision that seemed perfectly reasonable during pregnancy seems completely untenable after baby arrives.

The options for child care can be overwhelming. These include commercial child care centers, home-based child care (e.g., one child care provider watching a few babies in her home), nannies (e.g., one child care provider who watches only your baby in your own home), and family members (e.g., a relative who watches your baby in your own home or theirs). Although it is beyond the scope of this book to discuss the pros and cons of each, the bottom line is just that—there are pros and cons to each, and this reality means that one option rarely stands out as the clear winner. The decision-making process can become more complex when mom and dad come into their roles as parents with distinctly different opinions on who should be caring for baby.

It goes without saying that the working moms have to **balance** a great deal. Although today's fathers tend to be really involved and dedicated to their new roles, the reality is that moms tend to do more child care and household-related tasks than dads. Particularly for women who have always had high standards for themselves, it is jarring to suddenly realize that it is simply impossible to do everything "perfectly" while working, raising a child, maintaining a home, cooking meals, keeping up with friends and family members, and maybe doing something for oneself such as exercising or pursuing a hobby.

There is no doubt that, to maintain their sanity, new dads also need to learn how to balance new responsibilities and how to adjust their standards. However, the problem of balance often seems more pronounced for moms. Many women remark on how their husbands' work lives tend to remain reasonably the same after their babies arrive, while their own changes immensely. In the Calm Moms Survey, many new moms explained that they had made significant adjustments in their work lives after giving birth, such as switching from full-time to part-time work or accepting a less pressure-laden job. Moms also tended to be the ones to get their children ready in the morning and pick them up at the end of the day. Mothers tended to be the ones to stay home when their little ones are too sick to go to day care or when the nanny goes on vacation. Obviously, division of responsibility varies greatly from family to family and is not necessarily divided along gender lines. Regardless, when one spouse believes they have made more adjustments in their career lives than

149

their partner in parenting, a feeling of resentment can build. A sense of inequity can even cause resentment toward the baby.

A related issue is that working moms meet all sorts of new challenges in the realm of **communication.** Suddenly, one's personal life becomes relevant in the workplace as maternity leave and schedules must be discussed with the boss. Working moms also have to learn how to communicate effectively with their child care providers. These conversations might be about money, schedules, and vacation time or about more emotional issues such as how moms want their infants fed or put to sleep. Women who typically avoid making requests or asking other people to change their behavior (passive communicators) worry that if they do so, they will be judged negatively. Women who tend to blow up at people when they are trying to get their needs met (aggressive communicators) might worry that their style will backfire and have a negative impact on their child (i.e., the caregiver will hold mom's style against the baby). New moms quickly realize the importance of communicating effectively, even if it means doing so in ways that don't come naturally.

Two other challenges associated with being a working mom deserve mention. First, working moms frequently describe **feelings of guilt.** Guilt can pop up in so many ways. We feel guilty for leaving our baby's formative years to others. We worry that we will miss the first step or the first word. We worry that another person will not care for our babies quite as carefully as we would. Some moms feel guilty for *wanting* to work. Some working women doubt their abilities as a mom. We feel that because we do not spend every moment of the day with our children, we are less competent at caring for them and less skilled at playing with them. These doubts are exacerbated when the few hours per day that working moms do have at home with their little ones are less than perfect.

Finally, being a working mom can be **isolating.** Stay-at-home moms have ample opportunity to meet other stay-at-home moms. It is more difficult for working moms to meet one another. This can mean that working moms have few people in their lives who really understand what they are going through and who can offer valuable advice and emotional support based on their own experiences.

The Solutions

Fortunately, there are solutions that can resolve the challenges of being a working mother. Let's consider each in turn.

MAKE DECISIONS IN A STRATEGIC WAY. In chapter 3 I introduce The Calm Mom Approach to Making Decisions. There is perhaps no other arena of parenting in which this method will be more helpful than issues of work and child care. As I have noted, there are so many options for both—working full or part time, nanny or day care, and so on. Decisions can be so overwhelming that parents avoid making them or come to snap decisions simply to avoid all the anxiety of really thinking things through. Take time to make decisions and do so strategically. Sit down with your partner and brainstorm potential solutions (see the example of Lori and Jeff in chap. 3). Then weigh the pros and cons of each, come up with a plan, and set a deadline for when you will re-evaluate the plan and consider whether it is working out for both of you and for your little one.

This last step in the process is often overlooked, but it is essential. Setting a deadline like this ensures that parents don't become complacent ("Well, I *guess* it will do") or don't fall into the trap of feeling ashamed about a decision but sticking with it to save face. Setting a deadline for re-evaluation also prevents parents from jumping to premature conclusions about how a plan is going. Will you think your baby's day care is great the first day you drop off your little one? Highly unlikely. Give it 3 months, then re-evaluate your decision; this makes more sense. Obviously, this rule can be broken in the case of extenuating circumstances. If you stop home in the middle of the day and find your nanny in a compromising position with her boyfriend on your living room couch, I give you permission to fire her on the spot. But apart from an extreme example such as this, it is worth giving most arrangements a fair chance. As you get used to leaving your child, you will be able to focus more on the benefits she or he gets during time away from you, rather than on your guilt.

NOTHING IS PERMANENT. One of the most daunting aspects of making decisions about work and child care is that we tend to see our decisions as permanent. We feel pressured to make a decision that will work for us and for our children for the next several *years*. Although there is nothing wrong with having some plan for how things might be long term, new moms must also appreciate that there are too many unknowns in these decisions to make one that will work until your child starts the first grade!

Decisions are more easily reached if we accept that they do not have to be permanent. Many moms who responded to The Calm Moms Survey had already made adjustments in their child care choices, despite having babies who were still young. Some moms had tried different commercial child care centers until they found one they really liked. Some had one arrangement for the first few months but switched to another arrangement after their child was less delicate and more aware of surroundings. One mom was completely committed to putting her child in a commercial day care until she learned that he had severe asthma. The usual colds that most children catch in day care over their first winter landed this child in the hospital several times. This mom needed to adjust her initial plans and arrange for in-home care. Some moms initially returned to work but then decided to resign and stay at home. Other moms who had planned to stay at home ended up missing work or finding the financial struggle too stressful, and they returned to work. What was quite salient from the Calm Moms Survey was that frequent change during the first year was the norm—not the exception.

The most important message of these stories is that switching plans does not mean that an initial plan was wrong. New moms should not beat themselves up about changing their minds and should not worry what other people think of them if they do. Even if you did not initially use the Calm Moms Approach to Making Decisions, it is worthwhile to review your situation every couple of months. Ask yourself whether your current plan is working. If it is not, consider other options. Getting stuck in the mindset that your first decision is permanent will leave you feeling stressed out and dissatisfied.

BE A CALM THINKER. The arena of work and child care is one in which being a Calm Thinker is essential. Let's consider the example of Joanne to see why.

Joanne is a dermatologist. After college, medical school, and residency, Joanne had committed many years of her life to her medical training. Although Joanne had been in a group practice her first few years out of residency, she had started her own practice just 6 months before getting pregnant with her first baby. Joanne had met her husband in medical school and he worked as an emergency room physician. His shift-work schedule afforded him a good amount of time home with their baby, but when he was working there was absolutely no way he could leave. Joanne and her husband decided to hire a nanny to come into their home to care for their new son. Joanne was adjusting to balancing all the different pieces of her new life and generally felt good about it. Periodically, however, she had a day that led her to question everything.

One day, when her son was 4 months old, her nanny called at midday to say that she was sick. Joanne's husband was working. So Joanne had to cancel many hours of patients to come home to care

153

for her son. By the time she got home, her son was sick as well—he was throwing up and had a high fever. He was cranky and miserable. As Joanne sat and tried to nurse him, her mind started running a million miles a minute:

- *He wouldn't be sick if I were at home with him.*
- *My practice is going to fail if I keep cancelling on my patients.*
- *I'm a terrible mom and a terrible doctor.*
- *My son likes the nanny better. He's never miserable with her.*

When Joanne's husband called her during a quiet moment at work, she burst into tears and said, "We should have never had a baby. This is just not working out at all."

After nursing the baby and getting him settled down, Joanne went downstairs to have dinner. She recognized that she had gotten into a terrible mood and knew she had to do something about it. As she cooked, she engaged in some Calm Thinking.

- *He wouldn't be sick if I were at home with him.* Do I have any evidence of that? I'm a doctor and I know about germs. If I were at home with him, he'd still be picking up germs when we went out or if we had play dates with other kids.
- *My practice is going to fail if I keep cancelling on my patients.* Isn't this a little dramatic? Will my practice really fail because I might have to cancel on my patients once in a blue moon? I doubt it. My practice is growing perfectly well. If it turns out that being in private practice gets too complicated with a baby, then I can rejoin my old group. Nothing is permanent.
- *I'm a terrible mom and a terrible doctor.* Would I say this to my best friend from medical school who is also trying to juggle a new baby and a challenging career as a doctor? No way! I had a stressful day and I am allowing this to color the labels

I apply to myself. If I made a list of descriptors of what it would take to be a "terrible mom" or a "terrible doctor," I would see that I definitely do not fit those molds. I am doing just fine in a challenging situation.

- *My son likes the nanny better. He's never miserable with her.* Is there another way of looking at this? My son is cranky and miserable right now because he is sick, not because he dislikes me. And I know for a fact that he can be miserable with the nanny too. Babies cry. He cries with her, and he cries with me. He also smiles with her and smiles with me.

When Joanne tried to put this together into a calming statement she came up with the following: "Balancing work and family is a huge challenge—some days will feel more successful than others and that's okay." Engaging in the process of Calm Thinking got Joanne into a more rational mindset that allowed her to focus on what she needed to do (care for her son and cancel her patients for the next day), rather than wallow in negativity.

Working moms should be particularly aware of two categories of negative thoughts: perfectionistic thoughts and guilt-related thoughts. Multitasking and perfectionism can be a dangerous combination. New moms must accept that it is not possible to do everything perfectly when there are numerous major tasks on your plate. Your house might never look as neat and clean as it did prior to having children. You might not make dinner from scratch every night anymore. You might have to settle for going to the gym once a week instead of 5 days a week. You might have to work a shorter workday than you used to, thus taking longer to accomplish goals. Accept that these changes are not only okay but are actually *necessary* when you become a working mom. It takes practice, but you will get used to doing a "good enough" job at lots of things instead of a perfect job at just a few things.

It is also important to do away with guilty thoughts about leaving your child in someone else's care. As I discuss in more detail below, having your baby cared for by someone other than you is likely harder on you than on your baby. A few caveats deserve mention here. Even the newest moms should trust their gut instincts when it comes to child care. If you feel that your caregiver lacks warmth, if you come home every day to a baby in a dirty diaper, or if your baby seems despondent every morning when you leave her and every evening when you are reunited with her, there could be a serious problem that deserves attention.

However, if in your rational mind you recognize that your little one is being well cared for but you still feel guilty about leaving her, do some Calm Thinking. New moms often take things too personally. Babies are often fussy at the end of the day, so if a working mom only sees her baby at that time, she may incorrectly attribute the baby's behavior to the baby's feelings about her. Remind yourself that babies are fussy at the end of the day. And that's that!

SEE THINGS FROM YOUR BABY'S POINT OF VIEW. Another way to deal with guilt about leaving your child in someone else's care is to try to see things from your baby's point of view. In the Calm Moms Survey, many moms made comments that mirrored the following: "My separation anxiety was worse than my baby's." When babies are very young they are not terribly concerned with who takes care of them as long as they are fed, have dry diapers, and get lots of cuddling. This reality can make it hard for working moms—when we are finally reunited at the end of the day, our babies have little emotional reaction to seeing us until they are several months old. Rather than taking this personally, recognize that it is perfectly normal. Before you know it, your baby will break into a huge grin when you return to her at the end of a workday!

As babies grow and develop, it becomes easier for us to see things from their point of view. It is easier to leave a child when he is excited to see his caregiver in the morning and is eagerly listening to a story when we return at the end of the day. Moms who responded to the Calm Moms Survey explained that their guilt about working tended to abate as their babies grew up and they could recognize advantages of child care. One mom wrote, "I believe my daughter's child care provides her with more intellectual, social, and physical stimulation than I could provide at home." Another wrote, "We have always felt that our child care providers love our daughter and that was really important to us, especially when she was an infant. I also loved the fact that by 9 months old, she had a best friend." As suggested by the NICHD study discussed earlier in the chapter, child care might indeed have benefits; seeing these alleviates some guilt that new moms feel when they decide to return to work.

It is interesting to note that many of the Calm Moms Survey respondents, particularly moms of little girls, commented on how good they felt about being positive role models for their children. They want their children to see that moms can balance career and family so this can be an attainable goal for the children in their adult lives.

LEARN TO BE A CALM COMMUNICATOR. I mentioned earlier that working moms face many new communication challenges—discussing workplace changes with their bosses, child care duties with caregivers, new responsibilities with spouses, and so forth. Particularly for women who typically avoid confrontations, these discussions can be very nerve-wracking. In chapter 2 I introduced three styles of communication: aggressive, passive, and assertive. The ideal is to be a Calm Communicator by using the assertive communication style as often as possible. Consider these examples.

To a boss: "I'd love to stay at work late tonight to finish the project, and I recognize how important it is to get it done by tomorrow morning. However, I need to pick up Jeffrey from day care. He goes to bed pretty early, so I will work on it at 7:00 p.m. and be in touch by e-mail until we get the job done."

To a caregiver: "I understand you have a lot on your plate caring for three babies, and I know how irritating it can be to have Emma cry at the end of the day. However, I would prefer that you do not feed her at the end of the day even if she is crying because I want to nurse her as soon as I get home. Usually a pacifier will carry her over for those last few minutes until I get there."

Communicating assertively is so effective in getting our needs and goals met because it takes into account the other person's needs and goals, too. In these examples, the working moms took the other person's needs and goals into account (getting a project done by morning; peace and quiet in a child care setting). Yet these moms were no shrinking violets. They made their needs known in a clear way—picking up a child from day care on time and nursing a child at the end of the day. To make the communication more effective, both moms finished the request with a solution that would benefit themselves and the other person. One mom pledged to work from home after bedtime to get the project done, and the other mom suggested using a pacifier to soothe a hungry baby.

It is important to be mindful of the beliefs you always held about communication. Have you thought that you will only get your way through aggression? Do you believe that assertive communication simply isn't powerful enough to get the job done? Or did you learn from your mother that women should be meek and gentle? Have you always thought that being assertive would be interpreted as being too bossy by others? After you become aware of your beliefs about communication, test them out and see what happens. Try assertiveness on for size *regardless of your preexisting beliefs* and see what the outcome is. Many women find that it feels a bit contrived at first—but that it works. With practice, you can adopt a new communication style that will serve you well as a new mom.

CHANGE WHAT YOU CAN ... AND LEARN TO ACCEPT WHAT YOU CAN'T. Assertive communication is a powerful tool to use any time we want to try to make a change in our current situation. We can use it to ask our boss if we can work a 4-day workweek instead of 5, to ask our child care providers to do something differently with our babies, or to discuss important issues with our spouses. Even if a change seems insurmountable, it is worth using assertive communication to give it a shot and see what can be accomplished.

The reality is, however, that we don't always get what we want. In the earlier example of Joanne, she was able to cancel patients and leave work (despite the loss of income and possible annoyed patients), although her husband simply could not leave when he was on shift. This meant every time the nanny was unavailable or the baby was sick, responsibility fell on Joanne. For months, this irritated her and led to some snippy comments to her husband after she had spent a long day at home with the baby and he "got to go to work." When their baby was 6 months old, Joanne recognized that her irritation was futile. Their situation was what it was and there was nothing she could do to change it. After she gave up her negative feelings and moved into a stance of acceptance, she actually came to enjoy days when their nanny was sick or unavailable and she got some bonus time with their little one.

NETWORK WITH OTHER WORKING MOMS. Being a working mom can be isolating. It can seem impossible to meet other working moms who are sharing our current experiences. Every waking hour is occupied either by work or by baby. Yet it is worth making the time to do networking. We can learn so much and gain great support from other new moms who are in the same situation we are. One resource is *Working Mother* magazine and its Web site (see this book's "Resources for New Moms" section). This Web site allows you to chat with other working moms and connect with those who live in your area. Remember that it is also okay to take a night off from parenting—even when you are a working mom—to get together with friends. Form a working mothers' group and set a date once a month to get out and gab. Compare notes on the challenges and share solutions. It will be a night well spent.

STAY-AT-HOME MOMS

The Challenges

There are many challenges facing stay-at-home moms. When women make the choice to stay home with their babies, they often go into it with **unreasonable expectations.** They believe they will love every minute of it and never have a moment of doubt about their choice. Because of these unreasonable expectations, it can be very stressful to experience thoughts such as, "Gee, I wonder what's happening at work?", or "I wish I could have a day off," or "I'm bored." When we have these thoughts, we assume that something is wrong with us. We think, "If I were a better mom, I would not be thinking this way." These kinds of thoughts can lead to feelings of anxiety and sadness.

Women who choose to stay home with their babies also tend to have unreasonable expectations about the company that babies provide! I fell into this trap. My husband works very long hours including occasional evenings and weekends, and I assumed that once I had a baby I would never be lonely again. Well, ladies, let me tell you—there is a big difference between the companionship of a baby and the companionship of an adult! The biggest difference, of course, is that babies cannot talk. My 2-year-old is now talking from sunup to sundown, and I have to say that this stage of development is the most exciting, hilarious, and adorable thus far. But we are years away from being able to have a heart-to-heart chat about our deepest emotions or from sharing views on current events! Given this reality, women who spend days on end with a baby can become very lonely. For women who are shy by nature or for women who worry a lot about venturing out with their newborns, this loneliness and isolation can quickly morph into depression.

Perhaps the biggest challenge facing stay-at-home moms is that **people underestimate how hard a job it is to stay home with a new baby.** Because of this, people neglect the fact that stay-at-home moms need help and support. They assume that because the only thing stay-at-home moms have to do is take care of a new baby (not a new baby *and* a job) they are managing just fine. In fact, stay-at-home moms might actually need more help and support than working moms, at least in regard to their babies. Staying home with a new baby 24 hours a day, 7 days a week is exhausting, and opportunities for breaks are few and far between. Furthermore, staying at home with a baby can at times be frustrating and boring.

Complicating the fact that others tend to overlook the needs of stay-at-home moms is that these mothers might be **reluctant to seek help.** It is common for stay-at-home moms to accept the idea that "all" they are doing is taking care of a baby and thus are not in need of help. Even without this erroneous belief, many moms are reluctant to get help because of financial concerns. When new moms are not earning a salary they may feel that it is indulgent to spend money on a babysitter. For some stay-at-home moms there truly is no money available to hire a babysitter, so they do feel trapped at times. Some stay-at-home moms decided to stay home because they or their spouses do not trust other people to care for their babies. They may have held the belief that only family members should care for very young children. When reality sets in and women see how hard the task of mothering is, it might be hard to change these long-held beliefs and turn child care over to others—even for a few hours. Finally, some moms incorrectly associate needing help with failure. One Calm Mom Survey respondent wrote, "I never had babysitters until my child turned 15 months old. NO HELP. I felt like a failure for even needing a babysitter."

Another challenge facing stay-at-home moms is a **loss of identity.** Keep in mind that over 70% of American women work prior to having babies. For many women, identity is tied to accomplishments in the workplace. Women derive self-esteem from holding a job. Furthermore, job accomplishments are typically measurable. We might feel good about earning money, or winning an award for workplace performance, or simply being thanked for a job well done. Yet being a mom is a pretty thankless job! We don't get paid, we don't win awards, and sometimes we aren't thanked until our children are 30 years old and are making a speech about how wonderful we are at their weddings! Many women find it disconcerting to shift from being a multifaceted woman, to "just" being mom. Many women feel uncertain about whether they are doing a good job in their new role as mom without the objective standards for evaluation that they were accustomed to in the workplace.

Many stay-at-home moms plan to return to work. Thoughts about **returning to work** can also cause anxiety. Women spend years building experience and reputations in their fields. Leaving the workforce for even a brief period of time can translate into loss of skill, loss of esteem, and of course, loss of opportunities. Although some fields are increasingly committed to welcoming moms back into the workforce after they have spent time away raising kids, many fields put forth the implicit message that if you leave, you lose.

Before discussing solutions to the challenges facing stay-at-home moms, let's consider the example of Abigail. Before having children Abigail worked in the marketing department of a fashion company. When she became pregnant, she discussed working part time with her boss. He vetoed this idea, and Abigail decided to leave the company. Having worked consistently since she graduated from college, she decided she would enjoy taking time off. Furthermore, she and her husband, Simon, both grew up with stay-at-home moms and believed that this arrangement was best for young children.

After Abigail stopped working, she and Simon faced challenges they never had before. Their major challenge concerned finances. Abigail had made a good salary. She and Simon had contributed a portion of their salaries to a joint checking account each month to cover joint expenses, such as their mortgage and groceries. They put the remainder of their salaries into individual accounts and had always done as they pleased with this money. This arrangement no longer made sense when Abigail stopped working, so they closed the individual accounts and consolidated everything into their joint account. The problem was that Simon liked to save money and Abigail liked to spend money. When Abigail spent what seemed to be an excessive amount of money decorating the nursery and buying clothes and toys, Simon kept quiet. After all, she was spending money on a baby they had wanted for their entire married life. Yet after the baby was born, Abigail kept spending. Every day Simon came home from work it seemed that the baby had a new toy, Abigail had a new outfit, or the house had a new decorative item.

Their financial stress came to a head when Abigail announced that she had hired a babysitter to care for the baby two afternoons a week. This was another expense Simon viewed as unnecessary— hadn't Abigail stopped working to take care of the baby? When he asked this question, she became extremely upset. She told Simon that he had no idea what it was like to be home with a baby all day. She explained that she felt lonely and sometimes even bored. Abigail also told Simon that she felt completely unappreciated. In his mind, Abigail was not working and should be frugal with money. However, Abigail felt as though she was working hard and deserved to spend money to make her life a little easier. Abigail wished they could turn back the clock on their financial situation and return to a time when she could spend her own money without having to discuss every decision with Simon.

Another challenge facing Abigail was boredom. Some days she found her mind wandering from the baby to curiosity about what was happening at work. She felt pangs of jealousy when her work friends wrote her e-mails about the office gossip and the new spring clothing line. Abigail did not miss working per se, but some days she just felt purposeless. She missed the feeling of accomplishing something concrete, such as launching a new marketing campaign. And she missed the kudos she got when something she created was a roaring success.

On days that Abigail's mind constantly wandered she felt a complex mix of emotions. Many of her friends would have loved to stop working when they had children. She knew she was lucky to do so and felt bad that she was not more appreciative. She felt guilty that she was not focusing completely on her baby but was letting her mind wander to irrelevant things. And finally, she felt confused. What *did* she want? Why was she waffling about a decision that seemed so right when she made it?

The Solutions

Let's consider some tips for stay-at-home moms.

HAVE REASONABLE EXPECTATIONS. Anxiety often comes when our expectations do not match reality. New moms often embark on motherhood thinking every moment is going to be great, then reality hits and bad feelings result. Abigail expected that she would love staying home with her baby. After all, she had worked all her adult life and expected that she would enjoy the change of pace and the precious time spent with her little bundle of joy. On days Abigail was not feeling particularly satisfied with her new role—or when she thought about her old roles—she felt immense guilt.

It is best to enter this new stage in your life expecting that being a new mom is going to be the hardest job you ever had. When reality matches your expectations—or when reality turns out to be better than your expectations—you will feel much better than if you had set yourself up with goals that are simply impossible to meet.

RECOGNIZE YOUR ACCOMPLISHMENTS. Remember, the job of motherhood lacks objective measures of success such as annual reviews, a paycheck, or thanks. This was highlighted by the example of Abigail—she missed observing the outcomes of her marketing campaigns at work. New moms can try to put a type of objective measure into effect in their job as stay-at-home mom. Was breast-feeding hard the first few weeks and now feels so effortless? Had you previously felt a panic attack coming on every time the baby cried because you feared you would not know how to soothe her, but now you take her crying in stride? At first, did it take you half of each day to venture out with your little one, but now you don't give it a second thought? Well, give yourself a pat on the back for all these accomplishments. Although others might not tell you that you are doing a good job, it is important to remind yourself of the fact that you are.

IT IS NORMAL (AND ACCEPTABLE) TO EXPERIENCE A RANGE OF EMOTIONS. Are you getting tired of reading this tip? Please pardon me for being repetitive, but this lesson cannot be emphasized enough. We have been programmed to embrace positive thoughts and feelings while ignoring or beating ourselves up over negative thoughts or feelings. Life becomes easier to handle when all thoughts and feelings are equally acceptable. Was today a frustrating day? Okay, so be it. Tomorrow might be a super day. As I said before, the extraordinary moments with babies are special because they happen in the context of a lot of stress, hard work, and frustration.

NOTHING IS PERMANENT. I introduced this tip in the section on working moms. It applies to stay-at-home moms, too. Many women plan to be stay-at-home moms but then recognize after they are in the thick of it that it is not working out. Some women really miss working. It is essential that new moms do away with guilty feelings about *wanting* to work. A woman who is content in life is going to be a better mom than one who feels resentful and unhappy. Some women find the financial strain of not working too stressful. If all the checks and balances are not measuring up, it is okay to make a change. Again, a woman who is constantly stressed out about paying the mortgage and getting food on the table is going to have a difficult time being a Calm Mom. Do not beat yourself up about making the "wrong" decision or about failing. Refer to the Calm Mom method of decision making, consider other options, and give another plan a try.

On a related note, some women, such as Abigail, are sure they do not want to return to work but still feel that something is missing in their lives. Abigail decided to be her own behavior therapist by keeping track of her daily activities and her mood for 2 weeks. Abigail learned a few important things from her monitoring. She recognized that she tended to spend money shopping online on the days she did not have anything planned for herself and the baby. On these days her mood tended to be quite low, she was easily distracted, and she often fought with Simon when he found out that she spent money on things that they did not need. She recognized that her mood was good on days she had plans with friends, went out to run errands with the baby, or attended her weekly exercise class. For years Abigail had been helping her friends when they needed to buy gifts for people. With her eye for fashion and design, she would scout out great gift ideas and make custom gift baskets. Recently, she had been asked to help some friends, who offered to pay her for her services. It dawned on Abigail that she could start a small business. This idea was appealing because she could do this with her baby in tow and the amount of work was manageable in relation to her other responsibilities.

Working through this process of acting as her own behavior therapist was truly helpful for Abigail. From this point on, she ensured that she and her baby had plans to do one activity outside the house each day. She also started her custom gift service and found that it helped with two problems. First, it gave her a creative outlet—but one that she had complete control over in terms of time and effort. Second, it yielded money that she could consider her own. Although it was nowhere near the level it had been when she was working full time, she found that she appreciated this small amount and carefully considered how she would spend it.

GET THE HELP YOU NEED. The issue of child care is covered earlier in this chapter in the section on working moms. Let's be clear—stay-at-home moms need help with child care, too. Notice the choice of words in the previous sentence—I did not write, "stay-at-home moms *deserve* help," or "stay-at-home moms *should consider* getting help." **Stay-at-home moms *need* help.** If negative thoughts are holding you back from getting the help you need, do some Calm Thinking. Wanting or needing a break does not mean you have failed as a mother. Accepting help will make you a better mom. Even an hour or two away from the difficult job of motherhood will make you calmer and more appreciative of all the special moments after you get back.

The example of Abigail highlighted an important issue— significant people in the lives of stay-at-home moms might not understand why they need help. Abigail's husband wondered why she needed a babysitter, as she had chosen to stay home to care for their baby. In such cases, it is essential to be a Calm Communicator. Many new moms either give up arranging for help after they get a reaction like this or lash out at the person who told them they did not need it. It is best to calmly take into account the other person's point of view while voicing your own needs and wants. For example, Abigail might have said to Simon, "It might be difficult for you to understand why I need a break because you do not stay home full time with the baby. I do need a few hours a week for myself. It will make me more patient and focused when I am at home. I understand that finances are a concern, so I will limit the babysitter's time to 3 hours per week and cut some expenses in other areas to cover the cost."

It is okay to think about your identity beyond being "Mom." Deciding to be a stay-at-home mother does not mean you need to give up everything you did before. Many stay-at-home moms use the time they have a babysitter to enjoy the same hobbies or volunteer work that they did previously. Abigail began to feel more like herself after she started her small gift basket business. For new moms who plan to return to the work force in the next few years, time away from baby can be used to maintain connections and skills. For example, it can be worthwhile to have lunch with former colleagues once a month or to periodically attend a conference, networking event, or continuing education program. Engaging in these activities is far from selfish. A woman who nurtures her *whole* identity, not only her identity as a mom, will undoubtedly be a calmer, happier mom.

CONSIDER YOUR FINANCES. Stay-at-home moms lose the income they made as working women. This can cause significant stress. Families might find it impossible to save money; on a day-to-day basis, they might feel limited in their ability to pay for help from others. Keep track of your spending for a month to see if there are places to cut expenses. Do you find yourself doing too much online shopping when baby is napping? Do you often order out for food instead of cooking affordable meals at home? Do you meet your new mom friends for a cup of coffee at a fancy coffee shop? These little things make a difference. If you stop for a latté at a coffee shop every day, this could add up to almost $30 per week. Consider whether there are places to cut expenses and reallocate these funds to giving yourself a break. For example, that $30 pays for several hours of babysitting from a local college student.

Finances are an essential arena for excellent communication skills. In the example of Abigail and Simon, their marriage became stressed because of financial issues. They came into the marriage with different attitudes about money, but these differences had not posed any problems until Abigail stopped working. After Simon became the only wage earner in the family, he believed he had more say in managing their money. Abigail became resentful of this because she thought she was doing the most important job in the world—raising their child. Although this did not pay her a salary, she believed she deserved to spend money on little indulgences without having to consult with Simon. She also felt uncomfortable about asking permission to hire a babysitter. Abigail and Simon recognized that they needed to spend uninterrupted time carefully discussing these issues and adjusting their finances. Letting such issues fester can take a toll on marriages. Some couples benefit greatly from seeing a marriage and family therapist who can help them navigate these complex issues.

NETWORK WITH OTHER MOMS. Staying home with a new baby can be isolating, frustrating, and—let's be honest—sometimes boring. Many women credit a network of fellow new moms as their saving grace. The importance of companionship is covered in greater detail in chapter 7. For now, suffice it to say that getting together with other new moms and their babies has innumerable benefits. Sharing common experiences helps moms to see that they are not alone in the range of emotions they might be feeling and offers opportunities to learn from others. Furthermore, getting together with other new moms can break up the boredom of being home with a baby by offering a change of environment and an opportunity to have adult conversation.

LOOKING AHEAD

Up to this point in *Becoming a Calm Mom* I have focused on the obvious people in the lives of new moms—their babies and themselves. In chapter 7 I discuss the ways in which moms' relationships are affected by the arrival of a new baby. Most attention is paid to the challenges couples face when baby makes three and how to weather this potential storm smoothly. I also discuss how the arrival of baby can affect other relationships—changing some and bringing out the need for some we might not have had in our lives before.

CHAPTER 7

REMEMBERING RELATIONSHIPS: THERE'S MORE TO LIFE THAN JUST YOUR BABY

There is an old proverb that says, "It takes a village to raise a child." The idea is that many people—parents, grandparents, teachers, and religious leaders—should have a hand in raising our children. When I started to write this chapter of *Becoming a Calm Mom* this proverb kept popping into my head. Not only do children need many people in their lives to grow up well, but new moms also need many people in their lives as they traverse the road of motherhood. Trying to do this amazingly challenging job on our own would be too heavy a burden to bear.

Although it can be a great benefit to be surrounded by people as we raise our children, relationships can also be challenged. The focus in this chapter is on a new mother's relationship with her husband. In our society there are many different kinds of families. For simplicity's sake, I refer to *husbands* in this chapter. However, the issues discussed apply generally to any relationship new moms have with the other parent of their child. This might include a same-sex partner, a boyfriend, a common-law partner, and so on. When a baby joins any relationship, that relationship changes in many ways, both good and not so good. These challenges, and the solutions to them, are the focus of this chapter.

A new baby can also have an effect on our relationships with people aside from our husbands. Therefore, relationships with family members (parents and in-laws) and friends are considered in this chapter. Although the addition of a baby can change our existing relationships, it can also present the need for new relationships. With this in mind, I discuss the importance of establishing new social supports after we become moms.

HUSBANDS

The Facts

John Gottman, PhD, an internationally-known expert on marital relationships, recently published an excellent book, *And Baby Makes Three* (Gottman & Gottman, 2007; see "Resources for New Moms" at the end of this book for more details). The book summarizes Dr. Gottman's extensive and careful research on how marriages change when a baby arrives. His work shows that after a first baby arrives, relationship satisfaction drops significantly for two thirds of couples. Couples find themselves fighting more, report less emotional intimacy, and complain that the quality of their sex lives has plummeted. Although young babies might seem oblivious to much of what is going on around them, this does not seem to be the case. Dr. Gottman reviews research showing that babies react negatively to parental hostility—when their parents fight, babies tend to cry. Over the long term, babies who are raised by parents who are unhappy in their marital relationship are more likely to show delays in intellectual and emotional development than babies who are raised by parents who are happily married.

Dr. Gottman distinguishes between marriage *masters* and *disasters*. One of the most interesting findings from his extensive research is that fighting in and of itself does not distinguish marriage masters and marriage disasters. All couples fight, particularly at times of transition and exhaustion. Furthermore, most married couples (both masters and disasters) fight about the same issues, and these issues tend to predate the birth of a baby (in other words, we should stop blaming our babies for all our problems!). The important difference between masters and disasters is not the fighting or what we fight about. Rather, it is the way we fight that makes a difference.

Dr. Gottman writes "Couples in trouble are critical, defensive, and disrespectful with each other. They are blind to their partner's point of view and they can't compromise . . . Their partners seem like enemies, not allies" (2007, p. 17). Over his years of research, Dr. Gottman consistently found that the strongest predictor of divorce is **contempt,** which is defined as "sling[ing] criticism down on our partner from the pinnacle of our own superiority" (p. 58).

In contrast, couples who are classified as marriage masters respect each other, speak gently, listen, remain open to the other person's point of view, and are willing to take responsibility for their role in a problem. Gottman (2007) found that marriage masters tend to deal with disagreements in a strategic way—by first saying what they feel, then using neutral statements to describe the problem (e.g., "the garbage has not been taken out," instead of "you lazy jerk, you never take out the garbage"), and finally, expressing what they need. His research also found that marriage masters often inject humor into their fights.

In the next part of this chapter I discuss the challenges that marriages face when baby makes three. We know from Dr. Gottman's research (2007) that it is normal for couples to fight—but what are the issues that couples are upset about in the first place? After discussing the challenges facing new parents, I focus on solutions that should help you and your spouse end up as marriage masters, rather than marriage disasters.

The Challenges

What are the challenges that stir up conflict between husbands and wives after they become parents? Our Calm Mom Survey respondents had a lot to say on this topic. Let's consider the most common responses.

Many new moms who responded to our survey remarked upon the **uneven division of labor** after baby makes three. One new mom wrote, "As an independent professional woman it was difficult to adjust to the realization that things wouldn't be equal. Even with a sensitive and progressive husband, it seems it is assumed that the mom will be the one to take care of things unless the dad is asked to do something; it may be that he doesn't think of the things that need to be done and is unaware. This caused a lot of stress." Even when both parents work outside the home, many moms remark that they bear more responsibility for child care than their spouses. These responsibilities can include feeding and dressing a child, organizing and managing child care arrangements, taking babies to doctors' appointments, and staying home from work when the baby or child care provider is sick. This often means that moms experience more significant lifestyle changes than dad does after baby arrives. Inequities such as these can breed resentment.

The issue of the uneven division of labor is more complex than it initially appears. There are many layers to consider. First, **people assume that women know more about what to do with babies than men.** One mom wrote, "Being the mother, I was somehow supposed to intuitively know just what our new baby needed (and how to soothe him when fussy). I was also responsible for finding a solution to whatever challenge we faced if I didn't miraculously have the answer." This puts a vast amount of pressure on women, who often have little experience with babies until they have their own.

This assumption of maternal intuition sets up differential roles for mom and dad. One mom wrote that she felt like the "project manager" of their baby! She noted that her husband "has a tendency to ask me about everything like 'what clothes should she wear?' or 'do you think she needs her diaper changed?' " Over the first few weeks of a baby's life, many moms can fall into the trap of actually becoming the "project manager." Because moms tend to spend more time with a baby, they do become expert more quickly on soothing, feeding, changing, and so on. It is only natural that new moms then want to share their knowledge with their spouses. At times, this process of sharing can be delivered by mom and received by dad in a benevolent way—mom has figured the little guy out and dad is eager to learn. However, for some new moms the process of sharing can sound as though they are **acting like the expert.** They might deliver their newfound knowledge in an overly authoritative way, making their husbands feel there is only one way to solve each baby-related problem—and, of course, it's mom's way! This can certainly put strain on a marriage. One mom described this perfectly: "When my husband would come home and 'take over' to give me a break, I would usually hover over him telling him how to do things better. The same thing happened when he would have nighttime duty. If the crying didn't stop quickly I would go in to offer help. This caused a lot of tension because he (like me) doesn't like to be bossed around and felt like I was saying he wasn't a good parent." Think back to our Calm Mom strategy of being your own behavior therapist. What do you think happens when dads get scrutinized and criticized by mom when helping out with the baby? They tend to withdraw and stop helping. The perception that moms do more for babies than dads can quickly become reality.

Beyond baby care, new parents experience other **role changes** that cause stress. One survey respondent wrote, "Suddenly, I had gone from being a career-driven person to someone who was supposed to stay home and take care of a child all day and my husband was suddenly in charge of providing for all of us!" Although new moms get the bulk of the attention in discussions of new parenthood, becoming a dad is no piece of cake either! Dads also have to navigate changes in their careers and might be under increased pressure to support the family, particularly if moms leave the workforce. Sometimes, the grass begins to look greener on the other side. Dads can feel jealous that moms get to stay home all day with the baby. Moms can feel jealous that dads go to work, which now appears to be more relaxing than dealing with an eight-pound crying machine. One mom wrote, "It seemed like we were each intent on proving that our own role was the harder one."

As discussed in chapter 6, when one parent leaves the workforce to stay home with a baby, **financial strains** can ensue. Even when both parents continue working, the cost of child care can eat up funds that were previously earmarked for fun things such as eating out or going on vacations. The arrival of a baby often means rethinking the family finances. This can be very difficult for new moms who used to work. When women are earning money they can become accustomed to spending money without necessarily consulting with their spouses. The time after baby arrives is often the first time in a marriage that a woman needs to specifically "ask" her husband for money. This can stir up all kinds of issues. Some women feel uncomfortable spending money on themselves because they have not earned it. Some women feel they need to hide their spending habits from their husbands for fear they will be judged badly or cut off. A husband might ask his wife if she really needs something she has purchased, which may stir up an argument about the woman "deserving" the item in question because she is working so hard as a mom.

Besides finances, parenthood brings up other topics that couples might not have discussed before. Each member of a couple comes into the relationship from a different background. Experiences in our families of origin color our **beliefs about how to raise our own kids.** This can play out in so many ways. With new babies, differences in background might affect decisions on baby care—how to get a baby to sleep at night, whether to breast-feed or bottle-feed, whether a baby should be cared for by parents or by a caregiver. The arrival of baby often sparks intense discussions about religious upbringing—particularly salient for couples who grew up with different religious backgrounds, or even for those of the same religion who observe in different ways. Toward the end of the first year of life, discipline becomes an important parenting issue that also highlights differences in upbringing. Although it might not seem important if parents disagree on how to discipline a one-year-old who is using a toy to hit his mom, it is. These seemingly minor issues not only set a precedent for the child about what he can expect from his parents but also set a precedent for how parents will resolve discipline-related disagreements in the future. Discussing these issues is important, as parents need to collaborate to make decisions about how to raise their children every step of the way. However, when couples bring differences to the table, these discussions can be a great source of stress.

Two other challenges deserve mention. First, new parents find it hard to fit in **time to nurture their own relationship.** Spouses can feel neglected by each other when all the focus and affection is placed on the baby. Suddenly, going on a date or out to do something that used to seem important before baby came along seems indulgent, if not impossible. Even having the important conversations just discussed can get lost in the shuffle of caring for baby and earning a living. Neglecting to make time to talk with one's spouse or to spend quality time with them that does not revolve around the baby can naturally cause couples to drift apart. A couple who used to feel very connected can begin to feel like two ships that pass in the night (literally!), at the time it is most important for the marital relationship to be strong and stable.

On a related note, many couples find their **sex lives** change significantly when baby comes along. Many physical factors contribute to this. Sleep deprivation can sap romance in the most amorous couples. If it is 9:00 p.m. and you know your baby is going to be up to eat at 11:00 p.m., would you rather spend 2 hours sleeping or having sex? Hormonal changes associated with childbirth and breast-feeding can also sap libido. Many new moms don't feel sexy or attractive during the postpartum period. There is all that postbaby weight to lose, leaking breasts, and for many women, pain. Many moms are surprised by how long it takes to feel as if they are back to normal after giving birth. Sometimes men have a difficult time understanding how long it can take the body to return to its prebaby state; they might put pressure on their wives to lose their baby weight or to become more interested in sex. Furthermore, all the emotional changes that happen within the marriage when a baby is born can interfere with romance. If you have just spent an evening arguing about the inequalities in your marriage, it is highly unlikely that you are going to be in the mood for love!

The Solutions

If you spent your first few months of parenthood fighting with your spouse, rest assured—there are solutions to the challenges you face. However, perhaps more than any other solutions introduced in *Becoming a Calm Mom,* they take work! All the challenges introduced above are complicated by a major factor—sleep deprivation. Many moms remarked that sleep deprivation made them feel edgier, less rational, and less patient with their spouses.

However, it would not be prudent to wait until your baby sleeps through the night (thereby allowing you to sleep through the night!) to work on your relationship with your spouse. It takes extra effort to rise above the effects of sleep deprivation to focus on strengthening your marriage. Dr. Gottman writes in his book: "The greatest gift you can give your baby is a happy and strong relationship between the two of you" (2007, p. 27). With that in mind, let's consider some solutions.

BE A CALM COMMUNICATOR. If you feel exhausted right now and can only absorb one solution to marital distress, this should be the one. **The single greatest predictor of divorce is communicating in a contemptuous way.** Even couples who were good communicators before having a baby can fall into nasty patterns when they are tired and pulled in 12 different directions at once. It is essential to be mindful of the way you are communicating with your spouse. It might make the difference between your marriage succeeding or falling apart. Furthermore, every time you speak to your spouse in the presence of your baby, you are setting a template for how your baby will relate to others *for the rest of his life.* If you speak to your spouse with contempt, you should be prepared to live with a child and a teenager who speaks to *you* with contempt.

New parents should strive to communicate in an assertive way. What this means is speaking in such a way that you get your needs met while you take into account the other person's needs as well. To illustrate, let's use an example one of our survey respondents contributed. She wrote that within a week of having her baby, her husband made plans to go running and out to dinner with a friend after work. It is reasonable to assume that many women might veer toward either passive or aggressive communication when faced with this situation.

Passive communication: "Have fun, dear. I'll be just fine here with our brand new baby who has been crying since six this morning when you left for work."

Aggressive communication: "Are you serious? You're a total jerk. Unless you expect me to be a single parent to this baby, you sure as heck better cancel that plan, pronto!"

Neither approach is going to accomplish much. In the case of passive communication, dad gets his needs met while mom is left at home seething, lonely, and frustrated. In the case of aggressive communication, mom may get dad to cancel his plans, but at a cost. She neglects his needs and subjects him to threats, and may even do so in front of their baby.

So, what's a mother to do? The first step of assertive communication is to consider the other person's perspective:

> "I understand that you would enjoy going running and out to dinner with Doug."
>
> Then, **voice your own perspective:**
>
> "It's been a hard day home alone with the baby."
>
> Next, **tell the other person what you need:**
>
> "We would really enjoy your company and help for the rest of the evening."
>
> And finally, **offer a solution** that might be acceptable to both parties:
>
> "Could you and Doug reschedule for the weekend when I haven't been alone with the baby all day?"

When I teach assertive communication to my clients, many remark at first that it sounds contrived. I encourage them to try it anyway. Using a formulaic technique can actually be helpful when you are exhausted and not thinking rationally. Furthermore, assertive communication works! After people realize that it often yields satisfactory results for all parties involved they are often more motivated to keep using it in the future.

CONSIDER OTHER RULES OF CALM COMMUNICATION. There are a few other aspects of Calm Communicating to consider:

1. *Make time to talk.* Don't try to have an important discussion while a baby is crying, the phone is ringing, and you are trying to make dinner. As impossible as it seems, it is essential to schedule time to talk about the "big" stuff, such as decisions about child care, division of labor within the home, financial issues, sexual relations, and conflicts with family members. Find a babysitter, go somewhere quiet, and talk about the issue with no distractions. If finding a babysitter is impossible, schedule an evening or time during a weekend nap to deal with the issue after the baby is asleep. This means a dedicated period of time in which you will not answer the phone, check e-mail, or watch a television show. This focus will be well worth it if you can work through an important issue in a collaborative, thoughtful way.

   Even if you and your spouse are able to squeeze in meaningful conversation on a daily basis, it can be helpful to schedule a major discussion at least every month (ideally, every week) to prevent a buildup of unproductive emotions. This "state of the union" talk can involve a general discussion of how mom and dad think they (individually and as a couple) are navigating the transition to parenthood and a more focused discussion of particular challenges. Couples can keep a running list of issues they would like to discuss. Each state of the union discussion will likely involve new issues and ongoing issues. For example, during the month that baby begins to eat solid foods, the state of the union might include a discussion of what to do when a baby throws food or rejects a certain food. Couples might want to think about their strategy for these challenges to make sure they are consistent in their parenting.

During this same discussion a couple should revisit ongoing issues. For example, if a couple has devised a plan for dividing household chores, they should check in regularly to make sure each person is keeping his or her end of the bargain and to make adjustments as needed (when there are changes in work schedules or demands). A clear advantage of this scheduled time is that challenges are dealt with in a calm, systematic way, rather than in the heat of the moment.

2. *Remember to listen.* When discussing delicate issues, it can be hard to really listen. By the time most people get married they have formed beliefs about all sorts of issues, from how to discipline children, to how frequently a married couple should have sex, to the ways in which household labor should be divided. Such strongly held beliefs can make it difficult to truly hear what another person is saying.

Here's a strategy to try with your spouse. During the time you set aside to discuss important issues, make sure to give each person *air time*. Allow your husband to talk about his thoughts and feelings without interruption. This is challenging—it means not interrupting to say, "No, that's not what I feel," or "You're just wrong," or "You just don't get me." Just listen! Then, reflect back to him what you just heard. The tricky part of this step is to leave your own emotions and opinions out of it. Simply state what you heard him say. Start out by saying, "So, what you're saying is . . . .". After you reflect back, give him a turn to *edit* if he thinks you did not hear him accurately.

Next, it's your turn. Give your side of the story (with no interruptions), allow your husband to reflect back, and then edit as needed.

After these steps, take a 5-minute pause. Really give some thought to what your spouse has just told you. Try to see his point of view. And then, give some thought to a solution that might help you meet in the middle. Take turns sharing your solutions (again, with no interruptions) and work together to formulate a solution that seems reasonable to both of you.

Let's consider an example. Despite getting a clean bill of health at her 6-week postpartum checkup, Angela and her husband Jeremy have not had sex since their baby was born 5 months ago. Jeremy often tried to initiate sex, but Angela turned him down, explaining that she was too exhausted. Prior to having children, the couple enjoyed a good sex life but rarely spoke about it. Both grew up in religious families and were not comfortable talking about such things. So the months passed, with each privately experiencing all sorts of thoughts and feelings about this aspect of their relationship. Angela and Jeremy finally decided to set time aside to discuss their sex life. Jeremy got air time first:

Jeremy: Angela, I am really unhappy that we haven't had sex since the baby was born. I am starting to feel rejected. I see you lavishing all this love and attention on the baby and it makes me feel like you have nothing left for me. I want things to be as they were before. I mean, I love the baby too, but I miss my relationship with you.

Angela: So, what you're saying is that you think we aren't having sex because I love the baby too much.

Jeremy: No, that isn't exactly what I was saying. I don't think anyone can love a baby too much! I just feel as though you have forgotten about me since we became parents.

Angela: Okay, so what you are saying is that you feel ignored since the baby arrived. And you miss what we used to have.

Jeremy: Yeah. That's what I was saying. How about you?

Angela: I miss what we had, too. I feel pretty confused these days. Some days I think, "Tonight, Jeremy and I should have sex," and I even get excited about the prospect. Then, when evening comes, I am just too exhausted to even think about it. I think that you think that I don't want to have sex. I do. I just don't know how to muster up the energy. I hear from all these other moms that their babies are sleeping through the night. And I get resentful that I am still waking up twice a night to nurse. If only I were sleeping more, I think we could get back on track.

Jeremy: So what you're saying is that you are too tired to have sex because the baby still gets up so much. But, I am also hearing you say that you still have feelings for me, right?

Angela: Of course! Let's take a break for a few minutes and think of some solutions.

(Five minutes pass)

Jeremy: Well to start off, I am really glad to hear you still have feelings for me, honey. I was pretty nervous that something had changed. I have a few ideas about things we could try. I know I have never gotten up at night to give the baby a bottle, but maybe it is something we should consider so you can get more sleep. Maybe we have to think outside the box on when to have sex. We always assume we should have sex at night. Maybe you'd feel like it more at naptime. We always spend naptime rushing around doing a million things around the house. Maybe once in a while we should dedicate naptime to us.

Angela: My idea was a little different. I was thinking we could just table the whole issue of sex until the baby is sleeping through the night.

Jeremy: Angela, I hear what you're saying. But, I also hear from friends that some babies don't sleep through the night until they are a year old! I don't think it is healthy for our relationship to put things off for that long!

Angela: I see your point. Okay, let's try your idea. Certainly sounds like a more relaxing use of naptime than doing the laundry!

As with assertive communication, using the air time method can seem contrived at first. But particularly when people are sleep deprived, a formulaic method such as this can be helpful. It ensures that each person is not only heard but also understood. It helps couples to find solutions to challenges that take into account each person's thoughts and feelings, rather than only one person getting what he or she needs.

3. *Treat your spouse with respect.* Manners can fly out the window when people are tired, frustrated, and overwhelmed. Keep in mind that saying *thank you* can reward you in many ways. When you say *thank you* to your spouse for something seemingly little, such as changing the baby's diaper or bringing home a pizza for dinner, you are almost ensuring that he will do these nice things for you again! Everyone likes to feel appreciated. Furthermore, when you thank your spouse or give him a hug or kiss in front of the baby, your baby is learning to treat people nicely too.

4. *Watch your tone.* In all your communications, be mindful of your tone. It seems unlikely that any new parent is going to

make it through the first year of parenthood without losing her or his temper or using sarcasm. If you must holler, scream, or demean your spouse, don't do it in front of your baby. Babies do notice, they do get upset, and they are negatively affected in many ways. If you feel like you are going to lose it, leave the room the baby is in. Take deep breaths. Come back when you feel calm.

Ideally, you should not holler, scream, or demean your spouse even when your baby is not in the room. Communicating in that manner will get you nowhere with your spouse and will leave you feeling badly about yourself. If you feel as though you are going to lose your temper, tell your spouse you need to take a break. After you are feeling calmer, come back and discuss things rationally using the air time method suggested earlier.

LEARN TO ACCEPT WHAT YOU CANNOT CHANGE. One Calm Mom respondent, quoted previously, noted that she and her spouse seem to be in a competition to prove whose life is harder—the stay-at-home mom or the working dad who feels pressure to support the family. This is a common dynamic with new parents. Throughout our survey, many moms commented on how their lives had changed more when the baby arrived, how they had more responsibilities to balance, how they had more pressure to be the "perfect" parent. All this might in fact be true. However, focusing on inequities accomplishes little beyond breeding bad feelings between couples.

Certainly, if your spouse is going out with his buddies after work every night and spending the weekends golfing while you are home with the baby, it would be worth using your best assertive communication skills to make changes in your household! However, if the inequities seem less changeable, a few strategies may prove helpful. First, take a step back to consider things from your husband's point of view. Yes, he "gets" to go to work while you spend 12 hours home alone with a baby. But your husband has stress too— pressure to provide for the family, exhaustion from sleepless nights, and time away from your new baby. Feeling empathic about the unique challenges that each of you faces can help you move away from useless resentfulness.

It can also be helpful to move into acceptance. Rather than focusing on the inevitable inequities that exist within a marriage, it can be more fruitful to focus on what you can control. When our daughter was born I sometimes missed out on things that were important to me on the nights my husband was working. It took months for me to realize that it did not have to be this way. My husband was always going to have to work some evenings, but I could change other things in our lives. Now, if my book club is meeting on my husband's work night, I arrange for a babysitter. If my husband is working several nights in a week, I invite a friend over for dinner so I can have adult companionship. My focus is now on the things I have control over, rather than the things that I can't change.

BE YOUR OWN BEHAVIOR THERAPIST. In chapter 2, I discussed how you can use behavioral techniques to shape your baby's behavior (e.g., helping him get back to sleep during the night on his own). You can also use behavioral techniques to shape your spouse's behavior. Do you want him to be involved in all aspects of baby care? Well, be mindful of how you react when he does get involved. **Hovering and playing the expert** often result in dads bowing out of baby care. Rather, let dad have the opportunity to learn about baby care, just as you have. If he is with the baby less, it will take him longer to learn. But he deserves the same chances as you had. This might mean a bunch of leaky diapers or your baby being dressed in a really odd outfit. But consider the cost of correction. When you play the expert, a dad loses confidence; before you know it, you will indeed be doing everything for your little one. Rather, let dad do his thing and remember to say "thank you"!

Related to giving up the project manager role, it can be helpful to establish guidelines about how you and your spouse are going to handle challenging moments with your baby. As quoted earlier, one mom rushed to her husband's rescue if he was on nighttime duty with the baby and seemed to be having a hard time feeding the baby or getting her back to sleep. This mom's actions were completely understandable; after all, she just wanted to get some sleep.

Rescuing can certainly work short term. Maybe the baby did take a bottle and get back to sleep more readily with mom. But, over the long term, **rescuing can lead to problems.** Dads can start to feel clueless and want to bow out of child care, leaving moms to project manage the baby more and more. And the problems only get worse as baby gets older. Toddlers are attuned to who does what in the family. Beware of setting up a scenario in which you are the only one who can change a diaper, give a bath, or put your child to sleep. This will certainly leave you feeling exhausted, and it denies dads and babies wonderful time together. And it will set up a dynamic in which one parent (usually dad) is the fun one who plays and the other parent (usually mom) is the one who insists on all sorts of horrid things, such as ending playtime for a diaper change. The bottom line is that if one parent is carrying out a baby care task, let him or her finish unless a specific call for help is made.

NURTURE YOUR MARRIAGE. New parents often feel it is selfish to go on dates and leave baby home with a trusted family member or babysitter. Nothing is further from the truth. A few hours away has numerous benefits. As already discussed, time away provides parents the opportunity to have important, meaningful discussions without interruptions. Obviously, dates should also be fun. They should remind you why you married this person in the first place and decided to have children together! A night away from the chaos of the new baby can spark romance and send you home with more patience to deal with inevitable challenges. A night away can be good for babies to become accustomed to having other people care for them so they learn that others can meet their needs. They also learn that when their parents leave, they always come back; this lesson is an important component of forming a strong attachment relationship. It goes without saying that kids benefit in innumerable ways when their parents have a happy marriage.

Keep in mind that you don't always have to leave the house to nurture your marriage. You can have a date right in your own house! Make sure to have evenings when you eat dinner when the baby is sleeping. Light a candle, have a glass of wine, put on some nice music, and perhaps serve something a little special. All these little touches can remind you and your spouse that you used to like each other before baby came along. They can also make a couple feel as though it is still possible to nurture one another despite the vast amount of time that is now being spent nurturing the new addition to the family.

DON'T FORGET ABOUT ROMANCE AND SEX. While we're on the subject of nurturing your marriage, let's talk about romance and sex. When you have a new baby in the house, all your kisses, hugs, and cuddles are likely to be directed at him. This is great, of course. But again, don't forget your spouse! If you used to give him a hug and say "I love you" before leaving for work in the morning, make sure to keep doing it. Kiss him at the end of the day. Again, these little things keep your marriage strong and set a good example of a loving relationship for your little one.

Beyond day-to-day kisses and hugs, new parents must also be mindful of their sex lives. The most important lesson for moms and dads is to allow ample time for their sex lives to return to normal after pregnancy, childbirth, and the exhaustion associated with having a newborn in the house. Although your obstetrician will likely give you the go-ahead to resume sexual relations at your 6-week postpartum visit, this does not mean you have to have sex that night. Even if you do, it does not mean that everything will feel exactly as it felt before baby came along. It is important for both members of the couple to have reasonable expectations. And it is essential that both are open with their thoughts and feelings (in other words, use those communication skills). Don't expect your spouse to be a mind reader. If you don't tell him what you are thinking and feeling, he will make his own assumptions.

It is also essential to set up conditions that are congruent with romance. Couples will be unlikely to want sex if they have just been arguing about the division of labor within the home, if they haven't showered in days because they are so immersed in baby care, or if the baby monitor is turned up so loudly that baby's every utterance is blaring into the bedroom. A precondition of a good physical relationship is a good emotional relationship. And for many years to come, another precondition of a good physical relationship will be the ability to tune out distractions. Unless there is a medical issue that requires constant monitoring of your little one, it is okay to turn off that baby monitor for a while and practice focusing on each other.

GET HELP IF YOU NEED IT. Some couples have a hard time working through the strains of having a new baby on their own. This might be particularly true for couples who were having trouble in their marriage before baby came along. The best thing you can do is to seek out help from a professional, particularly one who has a lot of experience with couples at your stage of life. Ask your obstetrician or pediatrician for referrals in your area or use the therapist locator on the Web sites of the American Psychological Association or the

American Association for Marriage and Family Therapy. You can also check to see whether there is a therapist in your area who has been trained to use Dr. Gottman's *Bringing Home Baby* program, which is backed up by impressive research findings (see "Resources for New Moms" at the end of this book). Many people fear that seeking help indicates weakness or failure. This is anything but the truth. Rather, seeking help shows you have the strength to confront and tackle difficult issues, and that you want your child to grow up in a home with loving parents.

FAMILIES

The Challenges

Before we adopt the cliché of criticizing nosy, intrusive, opinionated parents and in-laws, let's first point out that many Calm Mom Survey respondents wrote about the wonderful relationships they had with their older relatives. Many wrote that their parents (particularly their moms) were their greatest sources of support during the transition to motherhood. Some also noted that having a baby had added a wonderful new dimension to their relationships with their in-laws. Although our parents were caring for young babies many years ago, they can still offer valuable advice and plenty of support.

Not surprisingly, many survey respondents also wrote about the challenges posed to them by relationships with parents and in-laws. The most common challenge reported was the tendency of parents and in-laws to be rather **opinionated** (to put it politely). Let's consider the example of Beth.

Beth and Jack got married in their early twenties. Beth's relationship with Jack's parents was a bit rocky from the start. They were very opinionated, and Jack had a tendency to go along with most of what they suggested. This was challenging during the planning of their wedding, but over the next few years became less of a problem until Beth became pregnant. Beth found her in-laws to be rather old-fashioned. They frequently criticized the children of their friends who gave their babies hyphenated last names. They also believed that moms should stay at home to care for their babies, rather than return to work. Early in her pregnancy Beth tried to tune out these conversations, but as the birth of the baby approached she became increasingly anxious because she knew that many of her decisions would be at odds with the opinions of her in-laws.

Beth's anxiety was exacerbated by how easily her husband gave in to his parents' suggestions. She recalled that during the planning of their wedding, Jack went along with his parents on many decisions simply to avoid conflict with them. Beth opted to avoid discussing this issue with Jack during her pregnancy. She hoped that when the baby was born, Jack's new parental role would propel him to a new level of independence.

How wrong she was. The first conflict arose immediately after their baby was born. The couple had decided to give the baby a hyphenated last name (combining Beth's maiden name and Jack's last name), and Jack's parents were outraged. For several weeks after the baby was born they did not speak to Jack and Beth at all. Jack was so distressed during this time that he begged Beth to reconsider their choice; she refused, and eventually, her in-laws came around. At this time, Beth began to look for a nanny so she could return to work. This decision also sparked heated discussions with Jack's parents. When Beth and Jack were alone, Jack readily agreed with Beth on the decision to hire a nanny. But after every conversation with his parents, Jack would start to waffle and ask Beth to reconsider.

Beth felt incredibly conflicted about her relationship with Jack and her in-laws during this time. She loved her husband and felt terrible when they got into conflicts with his parents because it had such a profound effect on him. When Jack felt at peace with his parents, he was pleasant to be with and was an involved, loving dad. But when he got into a conflict with them, he became sad and withdrawn. Beth learned that her day-to-day life could be made more pleasant by giving in, even if it meant doing things she would not do on her own accord. At the same time, however, Jack's tendency to go along with everything his parents said was incredibly frustrating. On rough days Beth wondered why Jack got married at all if he did not want to grow up and move away from the influence of his parents.

With respect to her in-laws, Beth also felt conflicted. They clearly loved their son and their new grandchild. They were financially generous, helping out with many expenses associated with a new baby. They were also generous with their time, offering to babysit on Saturday nights so Beth and Jack could go out or on weekday afternoons so Beth could have a nap. Beth understood that they were from a different generation and were entitled to their opinions. She was concerned, however, with the disapproval they expressed when she and Jack did not agree with these opinions. Beth did not want to feel that she and Jack had to pass all their parenting decisions by Jack's parents for their stamp of approval.

Although the example of Beth and Jack is somewhat extreme, most parents and in-laws will dole out advice. The arrival of a grandchild sets up a sort of mentoring relationship—parents and in-laws have already raised children and believe (often quite rightfully) that they have valuable lessons to share on the subject. Things get complicated, however, if parents and in-laws have negative reactions when their advice is not taken. Things get even messier (as in the case of Beth and Jack) if new parents are divided on how to handle advice. One mom who responded to our Calm Moms Survey summarized this issue succinctly: "The most challenging part of these issues has been communicating with my husband about my frustration without creating a rift between us."

Another difficulty that often comes up with parents and in-laws is **degree of involvement** with the grandchildren. Many survey respondents complained about family over-involvement— grandparents who drop by without notice, want to see the baby every day regardless of convenience to the baby and her parents, or want to take care of the baby on their own for extended periods of time. Although this might sound heavenly after a few sleepless nights, some moms remarked that they did not trust their parents or in-laws to care for the baby. Some were concerned about the safety of grandma and grandpa's house, some with the physical or mental abilities of older grandparents, and some simply did not want to be apart from their baby for more than an hour or two at a time! Other new moms wrote that they were disappointed that their parents were not more available to be involved with the new grandchild. One mom said that whenever she asked her mom to babysit, her mother would not give her a straight answer until the last minute, after she was sure that more exciting social plans hadn't come up.

Finally, the arrival of a new baby can cause stress to a family because **a baby changes the dynamic of the whole family.** Particularly when there has not been a baby around for years, families might forget about the limitations a baby puts on everyone's lives. Even if grandparents are visiting for one day, babies still need a nap, stealing precious visiting time! Babies don't behave well when a holiday dinner begins at 8:00 p.m. if they are usually in bed at 7:00 p.m. Babies who are at the height of stranger anxiety might not want to be cuddled by a relative they haven't seen in months. In these situations, blame is often assigned to new parents—they are too rigid, they coddle their baby too much, and so on. This leaves parents feeling uncertain about who should be flexible during family gatherings— their babies or their families.

The Solutions

Because so many people are involved in family situations, the solutions are far from simple. However, using simple strategies can make a profound difference:

BE A CALM COMMUNICATOR. In the case of family members, two areas of Calm Communication are essential: communicating with family members and communicating with your spouse about family issues. The Calm Communication skills that are discussed throughout *Becoming a Calm Mom* work well in both. Remember to (a) consider the other person's perspective, (b) voice your own perspective, (c) tell the other person what you need, and (d) offer a solution that might be acceptable to both parties.

Let's return to Beth and Jack and consider a few examples of Calm Communicating.

- *To Jack:* Honey, you know I am appreciative of everything your parents do for us and how much they care for the baby. But, I need us to make decisions about his care on our own. I need you to consider my views and I'd like to consider yours. Perhaps we can start by setting aside a specific time to discuss my return to work and childcare options.
- *To In-Laws:* I understand that your preference is for me to stay home with the baby. However, it is very important for me to go back to work. I get a lot of joy out of my work and we really need my income. Jack and I need to make this decision on our own. I hope you come to see that we will make very good choices for the baby and always put his happiness and safety first.

A few points deserve mention. Although family issues can rankle, it is important to always take a deep breath and take a minute to plan an assertive response. If you act on emotion, it is more likely you will lapse into either passive or aggressive communication. Taking the extra minute to think through an assertive response increases the likelihood that all parties involved will feel that their needs have been met.

Couples should consider whether every issue that is brought up by a parent or in-law even needs to be discussed. One survey respondent explained that when her in-laws would voice an opinion on raising babies that she and her husband had already resolved, she initially got into debates with them. She would try to explain her point of view; her mother-in-law would counter with her own point of view, and on it would go. The same debates tended to come up over and over again. Finally, this mom realized that "the most successful strategy was deflecting annoying comments and redirecting to other topics." In essence, she used behavioral strategies—by not responding to topics she did not want to discuss she discouraged future discussion of these same topics.

Perhaps most important, issues with parents and in-laws are unlikely to be resolved until a couple resolves their own issues. Couples need to put up a united front. In the case of Jack and Beth, Jack tended to agree with everything his parents said. So when Beth disagreed with one of their opinions, they criticized her for not going along with her husband's desires. When Jack came home from work at the end of the day, he and Beth would spend most of their evening arguing about whose side Jack was on, rather than enjoying the baby. Clearly, the only way Jack and Beth could weather this storm was to resolve who was going to be responsible for decisions about rearing their child and then deliver a clear, consistent message to others who were exerting undue influence.

At times family issues can be difficult for couples to work through on their own. Although family issues can become particularly salient when a baby is born, they tend to emerge from years of earlier problems. Jack never learned to stand up to his parents. They had always made decisions for him, from where he went to college, to what his major was, to what part of the city he lived in. When Jack got married, his parents continued to have this influence over him. Jack feared standing up to them. Jack's father's own parents had disowned him when he got married. They disapproved of Jack's mother because she was from a different religious and social background. From a very young age Jack had so feared losing his parents' love and support (emotional and financial) that he tended to go along with everything that they said. When he got married, Beth encouraged him to start making his own decisions. His fear of displeasing his parents was so long-standing, however, that he ended up acting dogmatically toward Beth by insisting she go along with their suggestions, just as he always had. A few months into their lives as parents, Jack and Beth's marriage was at great risk of dissolving.

It can be difficult for couples to work through these kinds of issues on their own. One member of the couple might need to enter individual therapy to work through issues that existed years before meeting the spouse. Of course, couples therapy can also be of great benefit. As already noted, seeking help is not a sign of weakness, but rather a crucial tool for strengthening your marriage and family for years to come.

CHANGE WHAT YOU CAN AND ACCEPT WHAT YOU CAN'T. Some new parents can become so exasperated by parents and in-laws that they become tempted to avoid them completely. This is rarely a good solution, particularly because it is important that children have relationships with extended family members. It can help to learn to accept what you cannot change and place your efforts on things that you can change. One mom wrote that her in-laws were constantly buying things for her baby. After trying to curb this behavior and failing, the mom decided to graciously accept everything her mother-in-law brought over and then donate what she did not need or like to charity. The mom who wrote about her social butterfly parents who rarely committed to babysitting in advance started to give her parents a day by which she needed to know their decision. If they were still on the fence by that day, she would find another babysitter—despite knowing that her parents would feel offended if they did end up being free but were no longer needed to watch the baby.

FOCUS ON THE POSITIVE. There is no doubt that people tend to focus on the annoyances involved with family relationships. It can be helpful to shift focus to what is good about family relationships. As already noted, it is good for children to have relationships with their extended families. Even if your mother-in-law irritates you, during her visits try to focus on your baby's reaction. Does your baby love being held and read to by grandma? Focusing on the pleasure in your baby's eyes can make a visit much easier to handle. Do you find your own mother overbearing and opinionated but have fond memories of her delicious cooking? During visits, ask her to show you (and the baby) how to cook a favorite dish.

FRIENDS

The Challenges

Long-standing friendships can also take a hit when baby makes three. The simple truth is there is **little time to spare** when caring for a newborn, nurturing a marriage, and for some women, maintaining a career. Spending time with friends can seem like a luxury or an indulgence that takes time away from more important things—namely, baby and family. Although friends understand the limits on your time when your baby is first born, after a few months they like to feel that they have retained a place of some importance in your life.

Friendships can also be strained when friends find themselves at different stages of life. Fess up, new moms—do you tend to be a tad **baby focused?** When every conversation revolves around your baby's eating and pooping habits and when you recount in excruciating detail the baby's latest developmental accomplishments, your conversation can become tiresome, to say the least. Such discussions might be of little interest to friends without children or to friends whose children are not the same age as yours. Furthermore, these discussions can be painful to friends who want children but for some reason cannot or have not yet had them.

Because there is such a wide range of ages at which women have kids these days, it can also be challenging for new moms to find that they are having babies at different times than their friends. Having no one to share experiences with can be lonely and isolating.

The Solutions

There is no doubt that friendships require some adjustment after you become a mom. Consider the following solutions with respect to your old friendships, as well as applying them to new friendships.

BE SURE TO NURTURE YOUR OLD FRIENDSHIPS. No one knows you better than your oldest and dearest friends. Do not fall into the trap of losing touch because baby is all-encompassing. When you are in the thick of new parenthood, struggling with sleepless nights and long days home alone with a newborn, there is nothing so refreshing as taking a night off and going out with an old friend. Doing so puts you back in touch with who you were before you became a mother. Yes, it is fine to talk about the baby and the challenges inherent in your new role, but it is also fine (and wonderful) to talk about the things you used to discuss before having babies. After days with a baby who cannot utter a word, it is great fun to talk about politics, the latest celebrity gossip, or even the weather. And remember that all the focus should not be on you. Push aside your sleep-induced bad manners and remember to ask your friend how she is doing. How is her latest romance going? What did she do on her recent vacation? How is her work going? Not only will all this talk be interesting to you, but it will reassure your friend that you are still interested in her, despite your understandable focus on your little one.

CONSIDER YOUR AUDIENCE. I recently went out to dinner with a girl-friend whose son was born the same week as my daughter. She also has another son who is just a few months old, and at the time of our dinner I was just a few weeks away from having my own second child, a baby boy. Our dinner involved the following topics of conversa-tions: dealing with a 2-year-old's temper tantrums, moving 2-year-olds to big girl or big boy beds, adjustment of older siblings to new sib-lings, toilet training, picky eating, and whether or not to circumcise baby boys. We had a ball! Before we knew it 3 hours had passed! We both left our dinner feeling a newfound sense of confidence in parent-ing our toddlers, having shared solutions to challenges we had in com-mon. And I left with great ideas about how to help my daughter adjust to having a little brother. The night was a rousing success.

Picture for a moment how our dinner would have changed had we been accompanied by another girlfriend who had no children. The poor woman would have perished from boredom. The bottom line is to remember who your audience is when you are socializing. It is completely fine to tell a cute story about your baby or voice a frustration that you are experiencing as a new mom. But when con-versing with people who are at different stages of life, be mindful to keep the conversation balanced—even if your baby is the only topic on your mind. Besides being good for your friendships, a more var-ied conversation will also be good for you.

MAKE "NEW MOM" FRIENDS. With that said, it is essential that new moms make friends with other new moms. Spending day after day alone with a baby can be lonely and a little bit boring. Furthermore, although friends with older children, our own mothers, and mothers-in-law can offer great advice, the truth is that their advice can be biased by the passage of time. There is simply no replacement for people right in the thick of it at the same time you are!

There are so many wonderful things about having new mom friends. First, because no one quite understands what you are going through like fellow new moms, they tend to be one of our greatest sources of support. Do you feel as though you are having an unusual reaction to being a new mom? Ask a group of fellow new moms and you are likely to learn that at least one other mom is having the same reaction as you. Not only does spending time with other new moms provide a metric for normal thoughts and feelings, it also provides a metric for normal baby development. Although all babies develop differently, getting to know same-aged babies will help you recognize whether or not your little one is doing okay. Spending time with new moms also provides an excellent opportunity for learning. I cannot begin to count how many things I have learned from my "new mom" friends. When my daughter was very young, we were having a miserable time getting her to take a bottle. She would cry and fuss and take an hour to drink just a few ounces. It never dawned on me to try different brands of bottles until one of my friends suggested it. I went out the next day and bought one bottle of the brand she mentioned and it was like magic; we never had problems with bottle-feeding again. Fellow new moms can share information about these little details of parenting, fun ideas for playing and interacting with kids, and effective ways to resolve problems with spouses and other family members. Finally, spending time with fellow new moms and their babies is fun. It can be refreshing to break up your day by planning to meet someone for a walk or a get-together at someone's home. Before you know it your babies will be interacting with one another too, providing them with excellent opportunities for socialization.

Now that I have painted a lovely picture of idyllic afternoons spent with a group of fun new moms and their precious babies, let's talk logistics. Where can new moms meet in the first place? After you have a new baby you find that you see other new moms and babies everywhere you go—walking around your neighborhood, at the grocery store, at the pediatrician's office. Strike up conversations with these fellow moms! Once in a while you might meet a mom who thinks you are odd because you are talking to a complete stranger. However, in my experience most moms are happy for the brief adult conversation, and in fact, some of these casual interactions evolve into friendships.

Another way to meet new moms is to purposefully go to places new moms go—breast-feeding support groups, neighborhood moms' clubs, baby gym or music classes, exercise programs designed for moms with babies in tow (see "Resources for New Moms"). The Internet is an excellent source for finding groups like these in your area. Before you know it, you and your little one will have a busy social schedule to fill your days!

Although these resources are certainly easier to pursue if you are a stay-at-home mom, many offer alternatives for working moms, such as evening or weekend classes and meetings. As discussed in chapter 6, working moms also need new mom friends.

One point deserves mention before we move on. Establishing new friendships can be difficult for shy people. I have spent most of my career working with shy and socially anxious individuals, so I would be remiss if I did not include a few tips geared to this rather large population. People who are shy often fear initiating conversations with new people and, in the process of establishing new relationships, worry about saying the wrong thing for fear they will be judged negatively. These fears can be compounded by the presence of a baby—shy moms might fear that people will judge them poorly if their baby is the only one crying during baby music class or if their baby spits up all over the carpet at the home of a new friend.

Shy moms might find a few specific strategies helpful. With respect to initiating and maintaining conversations with new people, keep in mind that the perfect way to do this is to look for a shared context. For new moms, this is pretty obvious—babies! There are so many topics of conversation related to babies that can serve as the perfect springboard for getting started. After conversations begin, shy people have a tendency to become self-focused. They pay attention to whether they are saying the right thing, what they are going to say next, and whether the other person looks bored. Not surprisingly, self-focus is a conversation killer. Try to view the conversation as a tennis match—you volley one conversation point to the other person, they volley one back to you, and then you use this point to figure out what to say next. Staying focused on the natural back and forth of the conversation instead of on yourself ensures that conversations flow smoothly.

Even in the context of objectively successful social interactions, shy people still tend to believe the interaction went badly. These faulty beliefs are amenable to our Calm Thinking strategies. Ask yourself, "What would I think of a fellow new mom who approached me in the grocery store to say hi?" or "Would I judge another new mom badly if her baby was crying during music class?" By putting yourself in another person's shoes, you may find that you are a much harsher critic of yourself than you are of others. The most important thing is to not allow these harsh critiques to propel you toward avoidance. Give yourself a break and get out there to meet people. Your mental health will be better for it, and you will also be teaching your baby that social relationships can be a wonderful part of life.

LOOKING AHEAD

We are almost at the conclusion of *Becoming a Calm Mom*. In previous chapters we learned how to calmly deal with our new babies, how to deal with transformations in our lives as we moved from "me" to "mom," and how to weather challenges that can affect relationships when babies enter our lives. In the final chapter we take stock of our first year as moms. We consider all the ways we have changed and all the things we have accomplished during this challenging but exciting year!

CHAPTER 8

HAPPY FIRST BIRTHDAY!

Before you know it, your tiny newborn will be an energetic 1-year-old. You might celebrate this milestone by throwing a party, giving your baby her first taste of cake, or buying her a new book or toy geared to her current developmental stage. But what about mom? There is no doubt that babies change an immense amount in 1 year. But moms do, too. In this final chapter of *Becoming a Calm Mom* I talk about how you have changed and what you have accomplished during this monumental year.

This chapter is quite different from the previous ones. Questions will be posed that will cue you to take stock of your year. There are no set answers to these questions because the answers lie within your unique experience as a new mom. Rather, they are meant to encourage you to give yourself a pat on the back for your many accomplishments and get you thinking about changes you might want to make in the upcoming year to make your life fuller and more meaningful.

GIVE YOURSELF A PAT ON THE BACK

It is hard to remember what your baby was like the first week you brought her home from the hospital. Think back for a moment. When babies are first born, they are unsure how to eat. They have a difficult time figuring out how to ease into sleep. They have no control over their little limbs. They cannot make eye contact. Basically, they are tiny, delicate creatures who are completely dependent on their parents for everything.

Now, take a look at your 1-year-old. Most 1-year-olds celebrate their first birthdays sitting up in their highchairs, eating solid foods, and having their first taste of cake. Most are pretty adept at getting themselves to sleep. Many are pulling up and cruising along the furniture and some are even walking. Most make wonderful eye contact and can light a room with their smiles. They make lots of noise, and some have started to say their first words. Although still dependent on their parents, they are beginning to show signs of independence, feeding themselves, holding their own bottles, and playing on their own. What an amazing transition in one short year!

How about you, Mom? In the next section of this chapter I present questions to get you thinking about your own amazingly rapid growth and development over the past year. Get out paper and pen, and set aside time to work through these questions. Rather than simply listing your accomplishments, write freely, as if you were writing an entry in a journal. Try to articulate your deepest thoughts and feelings about your past year as a mom.

What baby-related tasks can you do now that you did not know how to do or did not feel comfortable doing at this time last year? Think about all the things you have done for your baby on a daily basis over the past year: breast-feeding, bottle-feeding, preparing and feeding solid foods, changing diapers, getting the baby dressed, bathing, playing, putting the baby to bed, soothing and comforting the baby when he is upset or ill. What about clipping tiny fingernails, taking your baby's temperature, or holding your baby when he is getting a vaccination? How did you feel about these tasks one year ago? How do you feel about them now? When new challenges arise with respect to caring for your baby, do you handle these challenges differently now than you did as a new mom?

What aspects of your personality have changed for the better since becoming a mom? You always hear people talk about how becoming a parent changes them. Articulating such changes is harder than simply saying that they exist. Give it some thought. Have you become able to multitask? Have you become more patient? How about less selfish? Less anxious? Have you learned to enjoy life more? Have you felt love toward another person that you never believed possible? Have you become more willing to ask for and accept help from others?

If you are working outside the home, what positive changes have you observed in your career after you became a new mom? Have you become more efficient? Have you become better able to stand up for yourself to balance work and home? Have you accomplished something at your job that would have been difficult any year, let alone during your first year as a mom? Has becoming a mom led you to embark on a new venture you never would have considered before having a child?

What positive changes have you observed in your social relation-ships since you became a new mom? In the previous chapter I talked about many different kinds of social relationships—relationships with spouses, parents, in-laws, old friends, and new friends. All these relationships have probably been challenged by the arrival of your first baby. Are you particularly proud of having weathered the storm with one or all of these people? What did you do that led to these positive changes? Have you established meaningful new rela-tionships since becoming a mom? How have these relationships changed you?

Now that you have written your answers to these questions, take a look back at your list. Review your responses as if you were reading responses provided by your best friend; in other words, give them objective consideration. The advantage of considering your responses this way is that it ensures that you are giving yourself credit where credit is due. Many moms have difficulties articulating their accomplishments. Some moms hold themselves to **excessively high standards.** For example, a new mom who works as a realtor might beat herself up for not selling as many homes as in the previous year, despite taking several months off during the current year to care for her new baby. Some moms also fall into the trap of **social comparison**—always viewing themselves as not quite measuring up to others. For example, a new mom might recognize that she learned many new skills in the past year but will immediately denigrate herself by saying, "But, my husband does them better." Finally, some moms can fall into the pattern of **disqualifying the positive.** Again, they might recognize an accomplishment but disqualify it with a *but* statement: "I have become calmer over the past year, but I still lose my temper every so often."

Have you caught yourself in any of these traps? If so, go back to the questions and revise your answers. Make sure to hold yourself to the same standards to which you would hold your best friend. Returning to our example of the realtor, she could write, "Despite not working for 3 months and spending the other 9 months of the year adjusting to balancing work and home, I had a pretty good year in real estate." Do away with social comparisons. Compare how you are doing now to how *you* were doing one year ago. Are you more confident in caring for your baby and more skilled in managing challenging interpersonal relationships? Give yourself a pat on the back for that rather than focusing on your perception that someone else in your life might be even more skilled. Finally, stop disqualifying the positive. Beware of the word *but*. It is important to acknowledge accomplishments (e.g., "I have become calmer over the past year"), even if there is still room for improvement.

SET GOALS FOR THE UPCOMING YEAR

Striving for unattainable perfectionism is very different from goal set-ting. As your first year of motherhood draws to a close, it can be help-ful to consider aspects of your life that you are less happy about and consider ways to make positive changes. Consider the following ques-tions and, again, write down your responses.

Are there any baby-related tasks that you typically pass off to your spouse or someone else because they make you nervous? Are there things you have not done with your baby because anxiety is standing in the way? Sometimes we pass off baby-related tasks or do certain tasks only with the help of another person because the task causes us to feel anxious. For example, I know a dad who has never given his children a bath—not because of laziness but because of anxiety. Some parents avoid doing things they would really like to do because having a baby along makes them seem too daunting. Travel is a perfect example. By the time you pack everything you need for a baby, trudge through airport security, deal with the annoyed glances of your seatmates if your baby is fussy, and try to get the lit-tle tyke to bed in a strange hotel room—well, it barely seems worth the effort. On the other hand, there can be delightful aspects of travel with little ones, such as having them get to know far-away family members and friends. Give some thought to things you would like to get comfortable doing with your baby in the upcom-ing year.

What aspects of your personality have you felt most dissatis-fied with after becoming a mom? Although many moms in our Calm Moms Survey were proud of how they had grown and devel-oped since becoming moms, there is no doubt that the strain of new motherhood can also bring out less-than-appealing qualities. Do you become easily frazzled and lose patience with others? Do you feel stressed out all the time? Do you feel as though you have become your own worst critic, always thinking that you are not doing a good enough job with motherhood and all the other roles you have? Have you become overly critical of others? Do have a hard time getting the help you need to make life more manageable? Spend time writing about qualities you would like to work on in the upcoming year.

Are there things you used to do before becoming a mom that you no longer do, but you feel are missing in your life? Many new moms come to the end of their first year of motherhood and realize that it has been a year since they last went jogging, read a great book, attended a sporting event, or got together with friends for a girls' night out. How time flies. Being the mom of a toddler will be no less busy than being the mom of an infant, but with a year's worth of experience under their belts, moms often feel more comfortable doing a few things for themselves. Write about the things you most missed doing since becoming a mom.

If you are working outside the home, are you happy with this choice or would you like to make changes in the upcoming year? If you are currently staying at home with your baby, would you like to return to work in the upcoming year? If so, what do you need to do to put this into action? Many women feel so busy and over-whelmed during their first year of motherhood that maintaining the status quo feels easier than making changes. This is problematic because the status quo is not always the route to happiness. Some moms who stay at home during their baby's first year end up really missing work. Some moms who work feel that they are missing out on too much with their babies. Career choices that seemed fine before baby came along might now seem dull or unimportant. Child care arrangements that worked out well during the first year seem poorly suited to the needs of a toddler. Now is a great time to step back and evaluate choices about work, child care, and your current balance of work and home.

What challenges have you observed in your social relationships since becoming a new mom? Some relationships do not weather the storm of parenthood well. Which relationships do you think could benefit from extra work? Your relationship with your spouse? Your parents or in-laws? Your oldest friends? Spend time trying to articulate exactly what might be underlying these challenges. Do you and your spouse not make enough time for the two of you? Do you disagree on your approaches to child rearing? Do you continue to feel there is an imbalance in who does what within the family? In addition to thinking about the relationships you currently have, give some thought to whether you feel as though anything is missing from your social life. Would you like to meet other new moms who are in the same boat you are? Would you like to reconnect with someone you lost touch with during the past year?

As with the exercise on our accomplishments from the past year, it is now time to take a look back at your responses to these questions. Review your responses with an objective eye. Have you fallen into the traps of perfectionism, social comparison, or disqualifying the positive? The idea behind this exercise is not to critique your parenting over the past year, but rather to identify changes that might make you feel happier and more satisfied. If you went back to work after having your baby but came to realize that you would prefer to stay at home, this does not mean your original decision was wrong. It simply means that as you gained experience in your new role as mom, your needs and desires have evolved. Try rewriting your goals using fact statements rather than value judgments (e.g., "I plan to resign from my job and take Sam out of day care" instead of "I should have never gone back to work. What a huge mistake. I can't believe how much precious time I missed with Sam when I was at work and he was in day care.").

With your goals for the upcoming year articulated, how can a busy mom see them become reality? Here are a few tips to consider.

Prioritize

It is not necessary (or possible) to accomplish every goal tomorrow! From your responses to each question, prioritize one goal you see as the most important. For example, one question prompted you to think about whether there are things you did before becoming a mom that you feel are now missing from your life. Try rank ordering your list from the most to least missed. For now, focus only on reintroducing the item you ranked as first in importance.

Some moms might find it overwhelming to work on multiple goals at once. Consider a mom who ended up with the following goals after completing this exercise: take baby on first airplane trip to visit grandma and grandpa, work on becoming more patient with my toddler, get back into running, switch from full- to part-time work, and try strengthening my strained relationship with my best friend. That is quite a long list of changes! If your list is similarly overwhelming, try rank ordering all your goals (based on the questions you just responded to) and work on one. This mom decided to first focus on cutting back her work schedule from full to part time. Focusing on one goal seemed much less daunting than trying to work on all her goals at the same time.

Be Realistic

It is best to set goals you can actually accomplish. Set yourself up for success! Did you love to cook before the baby was born but spent the last year relying on frozen foods and take out? It would be unrealistic to set the goal of cooking a gourmet, from-scratch meal for your family every night. Rather, set yourself a goal of cooking one gourmet, from-scratch meal each week.

Articulate Your Plan

Some goals are left unaccomplished simply because they seem overwhelming. The best way to get over this is to clearly articulate a plan. You might want to return to the Calm Mom Approach to Making Decisions introduced in chapter 3. This approach is most beneficial if there are various options that can all lead to accomplishing the same goal (e.g., if your goal is to return to work, but you are unsure of what kind of work to do).

Even for less complex goals, it is still important to make a plan to guide you. Otherwise, you might feel as though you are leaving on a road trip without a map. For example, one mom set a goal of working on her temper. She always had a problem with anger, but it had become particularly pronounced toward the end of her first year of motherhood. As her baby evolved into a toddler and started to get into mischief, she found herself yelling at him several times a day. At the same time, she returned to work and found it difficult to continue doing all the things she had been doing around the house. This led to conflicts with her husband, and she was distressed at how often they were arguing, particularly when it happened in front of their son.

This mom recognized that setting a goal of becoming less irritable wasn't terribly helpful. One cannot just flip a switch and be calmer. She mapped out specific steps toward accomplishing her goal: (1) Order a self-help book on anger this week; (2) read the book within a month and try to use its techniques; (3) if the situation is not better 2 months from now, make an appointment with a psychiatrist to discuss options. This mom had taken medication and been in therapy in the past for difficulties with depression and irritable mood. She knew treatment had helped her a great deal in the past, but given her time constraints, she decided to try working through her irritability on her own first. As it turned out, she did notice improvement after reading a self-help book but felt it was not enough. She moved on to Step 3 of her plan and decided to go back on a medication that had helped her in the past. An advantage of this mom's plan was that she set deadlines to keep her goal on track. Setting deadlines for each step in the plan ensured she did not get stuck in a rut continuing to do things that were not working or not working well enough.

Seek Out the Help You Need

The previous example illuminates the importance of seeking out the help you need to make changes in your life. You've already taken an important step by reading *Becoming a Calm Mom*. Yet some moms will find that they need more. We are fortunate that there are a lot of excellent resources out there. A mom who is still dissatisfied with her weight a year after having a baby can attend a commercial weight-loss program. A mom who is having difficulty balancing a challenging career with her home life can work with a career coach who has expertise with new mothers. A couple whose marital problems have worsened over their first year of parenthood can seek out the help of a qualified therapist. None of these decisions are indicative of weakness. Rather, when parents strengthen themselves they are setting the framework for raising happy, healthy, and strong children.

WHAT ABOUT BABY NUMBER TWO?

The final chapter of a book on motherhood would not be complete without discussing the possibility of having a second baby. By the end of the first year of their first baby's life (if not before), many moms are mulling over this decision. Should I have another baby? If so, when? What is the ideal spacing? How will I manage having two? How will my baby adjust to a sibling? These are questions that can keep even the calmest mom awake at night!

One reason this decision can seem so difficult is that babies change so rapidly. We all have weeks when we feel as though we have the whole mom thing under control, only to have baby start a troubling new habit or behavior (waking up in the middle of the night, developing severe separation anxiety, throwing food and rubbing what's left on the plate into hair) the following week, making us feel as though we are back at square one! During the good weeks we think, "Sure, I could handle another baby." During the rough weeks, we think, "Gosh, I can barely handle what I have. Maybe I don't even want a second baby anyway!"

Deciding if and when to have more children is a very personal decision. Here are a few tips, though, that might help. First, be prepared for unsolicited opinions from everyone in your life and then remember to take them with a grain of salt. Some people will tell you that the route they took is the only way to go ("I am so glad I only had one" or "Three years is the ideal spacing between siblings"); other people will tell you that the route they took was a colossal disaster ("I should have had them closer together" or "I should have spaced them further apart"). It is interesting to consider other people's experiences, but the bottom line is that a decision must be made on the basis of what makes sense for you and your spouse.

If you decide that you would like to have another baby but can't figure out the ideal time to do so, don't rely on feeling ready as a sign that it is time to have baby number two. When people are asked how they *know* if they are ready to do something, they often say that there will come a time when they no longer feel nervous or uneasy about the change upon which they are embarking. There are two problems with this mindset. As mentioned earlier, you might feel ready for a new baby on some days and might think the whole idea is completely insane on others! Furthermore, the best way to feel comfortable with a significant change in your life is to *live it*. Think back to your first baby. Would there have been any other way to prepare for being a mother besides becoming a mother and learning as you go? Certainly, having another little one will, at times, be stressful. Yet as with your first baby, every day will be a learning experience, full of frustrations and joys. Look back at your responses to the questions posed earlier in the chapter. How will your experience with your second child be affected by all you learned from the first? Undoubtedly, there will be many new challenges unique to having two children rather than one. But you now have many skills and a greater sense of confidence to help you navigate this exciting next step in motherhood.

Finally, let's consider some tips for moms who decide to stop with just one child or who cannot have more children. Constant questions about when you are planning to have a second child can be irritating if you don't want another baby and painful if you can't have another baby. It can be helpful to come up with a response that can be delivered whenever the topic comes up. For example, you could say, "Junior is so wonderful that we've decided to stop with just him!" There is no reason you should have to explain the thinking behind your decision to everyone who asks. Unfortunately, people sometimes cannot let the topic rest and might say, "But he'll be so lonely without a sibling," or "I've heard that people who have trouble getting pregnant the first time find it easier the second time." Again, it can be helpful to have ready a polite response such as, "I appreciate your concern, but we are really comfortable with our decision."

PUTTING IT ALL TOGETHER

As *Becoming a Calm Mom* draws to a close, let's summarize what we've learned.

Becoming a Mom Is a Process

Perhaps one of the most important lessons you can learn from *Becoming a Calm Mom* is that *becoming a mom is a process*. Babies change so rapidly. My personal experience has been that motherhood is an ongoing cycle of balance and imbalance, dictated greatly by these developmental leaps. As each leap occurs there seems to be a few weeks of imbalance as our baby grasps a skill or works through a challenge and my husband and I must adjust our skills to meet her where she is. After this period of adjustment, there is another period of balance and calm—until another leap happens and the whole process begins again. As a new mom, I found the periods of imbalance stressful. Sometimes I felt resentful—I would think, "Gee, everything felt so comfortable last week. Why can't we go back to that?" Now as a more experienced mom, I see these periods totally differently. I take a step back and marvel at my daughter's growth and development. And I embrace the challenge of figuring out how to adjust our parenting strategies to each new stage. I have become accustomed to persevering with a new approach for an adequate period of time to see if it will work and if it seems to be ineffective, shifting gears and trying something else. Seeing parenting as an ongoing learning process is exciting and comforting. It means that we don't have to do everything perfectly from the get-go. As soon as new moms do away with the goal of immediate perfection, parenting becomes much easier and more enjoyable.

Don't Let Negative Thoughts Get the Better of You

It is completely normal for new moms to have all sorts of negative thoughts. After all, becoming a mom is an incredibly challenging part of life and can throw a curve ball to the most confident woman. Negative thoughts only become problematic if you let them get the better of you. Always remember that you don't need to take your thoughts as facts. Rather, take a step back and ask yourself if the nasty thought has a leg to stand on. Most often, it does not. Reframe your negative thoughts to be more rational and move on with your day.

Accept the Good and the Bad

Another problem with negative thoughts and feelings is that we try to push them away. Although we embrace positive thoughts, we view negative thoughts as unacceptable. We tell ourselves to stop thinking about them or stop feeling a certain way. The problem with this strategy is that it can make those negative thoughts and feelings come back to haunt us, with even greater intensity and frequency. Don't fight negative thoughts and feelings. Let them be there, just as you would let positive thoughts and feelings be there. It is normal for new moms to feel negative about some aspects of motherhood. As soon as you accept this, the negative thoughts won't bug you or interfere in your life nearly as much. Furthermore, allowing yourself to experience negative thoughts and feelings makes you greatly appreciate the positive moments.

Don't Miss Out on the Moment

In my opinion, one of the biggest negatives of stress and anxiety is that they cause us to miss out on the moment. When we focus on what we are doing wrong, what we are going to do next, or how we are going to manage a challenge that is not even upon us yet, we miss what is happening *right now*. Get into the habit of focusing on the little right now moments with your baby. Accept the challenging ones (perhaps even with a bit of humor) and enjoy the delightful ones. Try to spend at least 20 minutes per day being totally in the moment with your child—no TV, no cell phones, no e-mail alerts, no thoughts about work, no dinner preparations, no worrying. Just get down on the floor with your baby and become completely absorbed in the moment. When you see how wonderful it can feel to be focused this way, you might find that 20 minutes of "mommy mindfulness" is just not enough!

Keep Practicing the Calm Mom Strategies

Throughout *Becoming a Calm Mom* I discuss the use of six strategies aimed at helping you gain greater enjoyment out of this exciting but daunting time in your life. Just because you survived your first year of motherhood and are now a veteran mom instead of a new recruit does not mean that you should stop using these strategies. Stress can get the better of us at any time—perhaps as our toddlers begin throwing tantrums, as we return to work, or when we welcome the arrival of our next baby. The wonderful thing about these strategies is that you can keep using them to help you through all life's challenges. Write yourself notes about which strategies worked best for you and tuck them into the cover of your book so you can have a quick, personalized refresher whenever you need it.

Congratulations on your first year of motherhood and good luck with your ongoing adventures as you continue to become a Calm Mom!

APPENDIX: POSTPARTUM DEPRESSION AND ANXIETY

In this appendix I discuss the very real and very serious problems of postpartum depression and anxiety. First, I describe "normal" psychological reactions to delivery, because most women do experience some unexpected emotions when they first give birth. I then describe the symptoms of postpartum depression and anxiety, and most important, I describe the type of help that is available for these treatable problems.

THE BABY BLUES

You may have already heard the term *baby blues*. Even though I am a psychologist, I was unaware of the difference between *baby blues* and *postpartum depression* before I started writing this book. I actually thought that baby blues was an inappropriately cute term to describe the experience of postpartum depression. It is a shame that I (and presumably many other women) did not have a clearer understanding of the baby blues, because it strikes 50% to 70% of all new moms (Miller & Rukstalis, 1999).

The term baby blues describes the brief time after giving birth when women experience an intense myriad of emotions. One moment, new moms are crying with joy over their precious new baby; the next, they are crying with complete panic over not knowing how to care for him. According to Gail Erlick Robinson, PhD, professor of psychiatry and director of the Women's Mental Health Clinic at the University of Toronto, some new moms experience tearfulness without even knowing what they are tearful about (Robinson, personal communication, October 18, 2007). Most moms are not terribly surprised by the fact that they are crying with joy. It is the negative emotional reactions that tend to give moms a scare.

What causes the baby blues? The biggest culprit may be our hormones. For several months during pregnancy, levels of estrogen and progesterone are at an all-time high. Following delivery, however, these hormone levels plummet. This sudden and massive shift in hormone levels is thought to cause the mood dysregulation seen so often in new moms. The baby blues tend to peak in severity about 5 days postpartum and tend to improve by 3 weeks postpartum, after our bodies become accustomed to these new levels of hormones. Dr. Robinson explained (personal communication, October 18, 2007) that the physical exhaustion of having given birth and the round-the-clock job of caring for a newborn can also contribute to the baby blues.

Consistent with what I discuss throughout *Becoming a Calm Mom,* thoughts are another contributing factor to the baby blues. When moms experience that first burst of tears or first negative thought about the baby or about being a mom, their minds jump into catastrophe mode—"Maybe I should have never had a baby," or "What's wrong with me? I should only be feeling happy now," or "I am going to be a terrible mother." Any negative emotion completely clashes with what we *expect* we are going to think and feel when that little bundle of joy is placed in our arms. This incongruity between expectations and reality can cause additional negative thoughts.

What Can You Do?

The best treatment for the baby blues is expecting that they are likely to happen. When women become mothers, they experience a wide range of emotions—from the expected, positive emotions to unexpected, negative emotions. If we come to new motherhood *expecting* we will have both types of emotions, our expectations and reality will be in line. When we don't find a jarring incongruity between expectations and reality we will be able to accept the inevitable lows as a normal part of the first few weeks of motherhood.

However, the reality is that few women are prepared for this very normal experience. The strategies we learn throughout *Becoming a Calm Mom* certainly help with the baby blues. Perhaps the best **Calm Thinking** strategy is acceptance. When you are in the midst of a crying jag or negative thought, say to yourself, "This is normal. Just let it be." Don't try to stop crying or stop having the thoughts. Allow yourself to experience them, just as you allow yourself to experience the moments of joy. If we stop fighting thoughts and emotions that we deem unacceptable, they are more likely to drift away on their own. Let yourself cry and when you are done, go about your business. A joyful moment is probably right around the corner.

Another Calm Thinking strategy is to remind yourself that **becoming a mom is a major life transition.** In general, adjusting to any significant new role is challenging and does not happen overnight. Although you may have grown up believing you'd feel like a mom from the moment your baby is placed in your arms, this does not happen for many women. If you find yourself crying because you feel overwhelmed, unsure of yourself, or questioning whether you should have had a baby at all, remind yourself that this is completely normal. Give yourself time to adjust to this new role. One reason the baby blues tend to recede about 3 weeks postpartum is that moms begin to settle in to this new phase of life and begin to feel more comfortable with the day-to-day tasks associated with caring for a newborn.

It is also appropriate to **be your own behavior therapist** at this time. Although many of the thoughts that come as part of the baby blues might be caused by shifts in hormones, this doesn't mean you can't do things to make your life easier. Are you crying because you are exhausted? Have a friend come over to watch the baby for an hour while you take a nap. Are you having negative thoughts because you feel as though you are getting nothing done? Make a list of errands your husband or your mom can do for you. Are you becoming emotional because you are finding breast-feeding difficult? Seek the help of a lactation consultant as soon as possible. Perhaps more than ever, this is a time to pay attention to what you need and ask for—and accept—help.

POSTPARTUM ANXIETY AND INTRUSIVE THOUGHTS

Becoming a new mom can make you feel as though you are riding a roller coaster. In addition to mood fluctuations, having a new baby can make even the calmest woman anxious. Do you find yourself spending precious moments when you should be sleeping listening to your baby breathe? Do you feel your heart racing if a stranger (with potentially germy hands!) pinches your baby's cheek at the grocery store? Do you turn around at a red light while driving to ensure that you brought your baby with you rather than accidentally leaving her at home? Well, rest assured, new moms! These kinds of thoughts are common reactions to the transition you are going through and the great responsibility of caring for a delicate and precious newborn.

One experience few moms are comfortable sharing is that of odd or unusual thoughts or images. By this I mean thoughts or images that pop into our heads that at any other time in life would seem completely crazy! In the first few weeks of motherhood, I repeatedly had intrusive images while I sat on the couch with my baby, thoughts about her somehow falling out of my arms onto the wood coffee table. One of my friends had intrusive thoughts about falling down the stairs with her baby. Any trip upstairs to change a diaper brought on serious feelings of panic. We have all heard about new moms who drive home from the grocery store convinced that they left the baby carrier, with the baby in it, on the roof of the car.

Although we may believe that the occurrence of this kind of thought is a rare event, recent research suggests the opposite. Studies by Jonathan Abramowitz, PhD, associate professor in the department of psychology at the University of North Carolina in Chapel Hill, suggest that three quarters of new moms experience intrusive thoughts (Abramowitz, Schwartz, & Moore, 2003). Perhaps a more interesting finding is that three quarters of new dads also experience intrusive thoughts. Dr. Abramowitz explored the kinds of intrusive thoughts that new parents commonly experience. They include thoughts pertaining to suffocation or sudden infant death syndrome (e.g., "Maybe my baby rolled over and suffered SIDS"), thoughts of accidents (e.g., "I think of the neighbor's dog attacking the baby"), unwanted ideas or urges of intentional harm (e.g., "Would she be brain damaged if I threw her out the window?"), and thoughts of losing the infant (e.g., "Someone stealing my baby in the grocery store"). Abramowitz et al. wrote, "Our findings . . . support the hypothesis that senseless, intrusive, unacceptable thoughts, ideas, urges, and images about infants are common among healthy parents of newborns" (p. 161).

One of the most surprising findings of the research by Abramowitz et al. (2003) was that both mothers and fathers experience intrusive thoughts about harm befalling their new baby. One might assume that these thoughts are caused by hormonal shifts following childbirth, but because fathers also experience them, other factors must play a role. Abramowitz et al. suggested that these thoughts might occur because of the overwhelming sense of responsibility that new moms and dads feel when they become parents.

What Can You Do?

There are two essential rules for dealing with strange or unusual thoughts or images. First, **don't try to fight your thoughts**. As soon as you try to put them out of your mind, reassure yourself that the bad thing won't happen, or seek reassurance from others, the thoughts are likely to increase in frequency and intensity. Instead, just let the thought be. When I experienced the distressing image of my baby falling onto the coffee table, I just said to myself, "Odd thought." I immediately got busy with something else (of course, there was never a shortage of things to do!).

Although you shouldn't fight intrusive thoughts, it is certainly okay to acknowledge that you are experiencing them and consider whether they indicate that you need a break. Remember that intrusive thoughts might arise from the overwhelming sense of responsibility new parents feel for their babies. If you are experiencing numerous intrusive thoughts, you might ask a friend or family member to come over to watch the baby for a few hours so you can take a nap or have an hour or two for yourself. Refueling in this way might, in effect, clear your mind.

The second essential rule for dealing with strange or unusual thoughts or images is to **not respond to the thought with a change in your behavior**. For me, this meant continuing to hold the baby on the couch rather than moving to a seat that was not next to the coffee table. For my friend who feared carrying the baby upstairs, this meant carrying the baby upstairs herself rather than asking her husband to do it. For women who fear leaving their babies on the hood of the car, this means continuing your drive home without stopping to check. I have never once heard of a woman who stopped to check and actually did find her baby catching some fresh air on the roof!

The bottom line is that intrusive thoughts can be greedy—as soon as you feed them by responding to their demands (e.g., by checking, changing behavior, seeking reassurance), they want more. You could then find that you are experiencing intrusive thoughts and images frequently and with great intensity. And you could find that you are spending much of your day trying to quell these thoughts by responding to them (e.g., stopping every few blocks to ensure your baby is still in the car). It is best to nip the problem in the bud—let the thoughts be there, but do nothing in response. If you try this it is likely they will become a distant memory of those foggy first weeks of motherhood.

For some new parents, in particular, those who have a history of obsessive–compulsive disorder, it can be hard to get a handle on intrusive thoughts without help. If you find that your intrusive thoughts are becoming more frequent, more intense, or are leading to significant changes in your behavior, seek the help of a therapist as soon as possible. For guidelines on finding a therapist who has experience dealing with obsessive thoughts, see the section on obsessive–compulsive disorder later in the "Resources for New Moms" section.

POSTPARTUM DEPRESSION

Many women experience mood fluctuations and anxiety in response to being new moms. These experiences tend to recede as hormones settle down and women gain some confidence in their mothering abilities. For a smaller group of women, mood and anxiety problems are more severe and more entrenched. In the remainder of this appendix I discuss postpartum depression (PPD) and anxiety disorders.

The *Diagnostic and Statistical Manual of Mental Disorders* (4th ed., *DSM–IV;* American Psychiatric Association, 1994) defines PPD as an episode of major depression that begins within 4 weeks after giving birth. PPD is defined the same way as depression that occurs in any other context. A diagnosis is made when a person experiences at least five symptoms of depression. At least one of these five symptoms must be either (a) a depressed mood most of the day, nearly every day for 2 weeks or more, and/or (b) a loss of interest or pleasure in things a person previously enjoyed. The other symptoms of depression are significant weight loss, weight gain, or a significant increase or decrease in appetite; difficulty falling or staying asleep or sleeping much more than usual; being very fidgety and restless or moving much more slowly than normal; feeling fatigued; feeling worthless or guilty; difficulty thinking, concentrating, or making decisions; and recurrent thoughts of death.

Looking at these symptoms, it makes sense that new moms might have a hard time distinguishing what is a normal part of being a new mom from clinical depression. After all, most new moms experience changes in their sleep, feel fatigued, and have difficulties concentrating. Because of this overlap, moms might shrug off troubling symptoms as *normal* and therefore might not get the help that they need.

Dr. Robinson (personal communication, October 8, 2007) suggested looking beyond the *DSM–IV* criteria for warning signs that might more clearly distinguish PPD from the normal adjustment to motherhood or the baby blues.

- **Duration.** The baby blues tend to go away by about 3 weeks after the baby is born. In contrast, symptoms of PPD continue past this point and often worsen over time.
- **Depth of sadness.** It is normal for new moms to have periods during the day when they become tearful. This tearfulness can be accompanied by negative thoughts about motherhood. Women with PPD also experience tearfulness and negative thoughts, but they tend to experience a "lower low" than women without PPD. Specifically, women with PPD often experience hopeless thoughts. A person is considered to have hopeless thoughts when she feels "trapped in a bad situation

from which there is no escape" and when she "views continuation in this situation as unbearable" (Beck, Rush, Shaw, & Emery, 1979, p. 215). For example, a new mom with PPD might think, "I should have never become a mom because I will *never* be a good one," or "I feel so guilty that my baby will have to grow up *for the rest of his life* with a terrible mother like me."

- **Sleep Difficulties.** All new moms have difficulties with sleep—namely, not getting enough! Dr. Robinson pointed out, however, that the sleep difficulties observed in PPD are unique. Moms with PPD often cannot fall asleep even when the baby is asleep and then have trouble rousing themselves when the baby wakes up and needs attention.

- **Ability to Respond to Baby.** Although all new moms might find themselves anxious or frustrated when things are not going well with their new babies, they can experience pleasure when the baby is calm and alert (or sleeping like an angel). In contrast, women with PPD often continue to feel depressed even during these objectively more enjoyable times.

Now that we understand the symptoms of PPD, let's consider who is at risk for developing it. Some women are more at risk than others. Specifically, women who had depressive episodes other times in their lives are more at risk than women who have never been depressed. Women with a family history of depression are also at greater risk. Significant stress or a lack of social support at the time of childbirth also make women more prone to developing PPD.

Although it is helpful to be aware of these risk factors, Dr. Robinson pointed out, **"the most common postpartum complication is depression"** (personal communication, October 18, 2007). This means every new mom should know that she is at risk for developing PPD simply because she has given birth—regardless of personal or family history of depression, and regardless of what is going on in her life at the time she gave birth. Although nurses and obstetricians might tell patients to look out for excessive bleeding or infection postdelivery, these complications are rarer than depression.

Dr. Robinson offered interesting insights into why PPD so often goes undiagnosed and untreated. She noted that obstetricians are often not well educated on the topic or about how to ask women about their emotional state. At the 6-week postpartum visit, obstetricians tend to focus on physical health. In fact, *Parents* magazine (2007, p. 107) reported that 79% of doctors say they're unlikely to formally screen new mothers for depression. Dr. Robinson suggested that this oversight is not because doctors do not care about mental health, but because doctors assume that a woman *knows* that she has postpartum depression and will talk about it and ask for help. Unfortunately, many women with the disorder erroneously think it is normal to feel this way or that they are just bad mothers. They attribute negative thoughts, feelings, and behaviors to personality deficits, rather than to a biological disorder. As such, they are unlikely to tell their doctors about how low they are feeling.

What Can You Do?

If you believe you might have PPD, contact your obstetrician immediately. There is no need to wait until your scheduled postpartum visit. If you already had your postpartum visit and did not mention your problems with mood or you feel that the recommendations your doctor initially made were not helpful, make a follow-up appointment. Your obstetrician should recommend that you come in for an appointment or refer you to a mental health professional in your area who specializes in PPD. You can also contact a mental health professional on your own. If you are in an emergency situation (i.e., you fear that you are at risk of harming yourself or your baby), you should immediately call 911 or go to your nearest emergency room.

Unfortunately, new moms are often reluctant to seek help for PPD. Let's consider some thoughts new moms might have and how you can use your Calm Thinking strategies to think more rationally.

- *"I am thinking and feeling this way because I am a 'bad mother'."* Calming Statement: "PPD has nothing to do with being a 'bad mother' or with any other aspect of my personality. PPD is an illness that I can get help with just as if I had an infection or another physical complication after having my baby."
- *"It is selfish for me to be complaining about my problems right now. My focus should be on my baby."* Calming Statement: "It would be selfish of me to *not* get help for PPD. Getting help will make things better for me, my baby, and our family."
- *"The doctor will think I'm wasting her time for coming in."* Calming Statement: "Doctors are there to help us. The only waste of time would be if I waited one more day to get help for me and my baby."
- *"I should just give it some time. I am sure this will pass on its own."* Calming Statement: "There are probably all sorts of things I can do to make things more manageable for me *now,* rather than just biding my time and waiting to see if I feel better."

The biggest hurdle in getting treatment for PPD is admitting that it is okay to take care of yourself at a time when another little human being is so dependent on you to take of him or her. After you give yourself permission to get help, you will learn that PPD is a very treatable disorder. Research has shown that antidepressant medication, therapy, or a combination of both are effective treatments for PPD.

Let's discuss medication first. Many new moms assume they cannot take medications while they are breast-feeding. Moms who are committed to breast-feeding might put aside their need for treatment in favor of nursing their babies. Be sure to discuss the option of taking medication with your doctor. Recent research suggests that new moms can continue to breast-feed while taking certain antidepressant medications (Payne, 2007). The decision to take medication is personal and even with reassurance from a physician, some mothers will not want to breast-feed while taking antidepressants. Again, putting aside your needs is probably not the best decision. When new moms are depressed they can have difficulty interacting with and caring for their babies. Research has shown that growing up with a depressed mom is related to negative outcomes for babies (Grace, Evindar, & Stewart, 2003). The best thing you can do for your baby is to take care of yourself. There is no doubt that you, your baby, and your entire family will benefit from treating your depression, whether it is with medication, therapy, or a combination of the two.

Researchers have studied two forms of therapy in women with PPD: cognitive behavior therapy (CBT) and interpersonal therapy (IPT). Both treatments were originally developed as treatments for depression and have been applied to other psychiatric disorders. You already have an idea about CBT from this book. This therapy is typically brief (16–20 sessions) and involves challenging negative thoughts and implementing behavioral changes to improve mood and functioning. Like CBT, IPT is also typically brief (12–16 sessions), with focus placed on the patient's interpersonal interactions and social functioning instead of on depression per se. The assumption underlying IPT is that by improving the patient's social functioning (e.g., which might include dealing with interpersonal conflicts and adjusting to new roles), the depressive symptoms will improve.

CBT and IPT are the only forms of therapy that have been systematically studied in women with PPD. Seeking out a therapist who does one of these forms of treatment is a good choice for women with PPD. However, other forms of therapy can be helpful and are definitely preferable to not seeking treatment at all. When selecting a therapist, new moms should consider two factors. First, it is best to find a therapist who has experience working with PPD. Second, it is important to find a therapist you like and with whom you feel comfortable sharing your most personal thoughts and feelings. A strong therapeutic relationship is usually predictive of good therapy outcome. Suggestions for how to find a therapist are given in the "Resources for New Moms" section.

ANXIETY DISORDERS DURING THE POSTPARTUM PERIOD

The *DSM–IV* includes six anxiety disorders, two of which have garnered the most research attention in new moms: panic disorder and obsessive–compulsive disorder (OCD). Although new cases of these disorders can emerge during the postpartum period, it is more typical for those who had the disorders (or symptoms of the disorders) before becoming moms to observe a worsening or recurrence of symptoms after their babies are born.

PANIC DISORDER

Let's first discuss panic disorder. *Panic disorder* is diagnosed when people experience recurrent (two or more), unexpected ("out of the blue") panic attacks. A *panic attack* is characterized by a period of fear or discomfort during which a person experiences at least four panic symptoms. These symptoms can include cardiovascular and respiratory symptoms such as heart palpitations and shortness of breath, gastrointestinal symptoms such as nausea or abdominal distress, and cognitive symptoms such as fear of losing control or going crazy. For some who experience panic attacks, the main symptom is a sense of

233

derealization (feelings of unreality) or *depersonalization* (feeling detached from oneself). Because there are so many possible panic symptoms, an attack in one person can look very different from an attack in another person. Panic attack symptoms come on abruptly and peak within 10 minutes. This does not mean that a panic attack completely goes away within 10 minutes; rather, the symptoms reach their peak severity and intensity rapidly and then recede gradually.

Simply experiencing panic symptoms does not mean that you have a psychological disorder. Rather, panic disorder is only diagnosed in people who experience panic symptoms and *fear* the symptoms, assuming that they mean something terrible is going to happen. For example, many people with panic disorder fear they are having a heart attack when their hearts race. Similarly, one of my patients whose main panic symptom was dizziness feared fainting in public. She envisioned people just stepping over her on the street or in the grocery store instead of helping her.

Panic disorder can be diagnosed with or without agoraphobia. *Agoraphobia* is defined as anxiety about being in particular places or situations where escape might be difficult or help might not be available should a panic attack or panic-like symptoms arise. Commonly feared situations include using public transportation, going to movie theatres, being away from home, and being in crowds. Agoraphobia leads to avoidance of these situations or great distress when in these situations if they cannot be avoided. A person is diagnosed with panic disorder with agoraphobia if they (a) avoid situations because of their fear of having a panic attack while in them, (b) endure such situations with a great deal of distress, or (c) enter such situations but with a "safe person" or by engaging in some other safety behavior such as carrying anti-anxiety medication, sitting near an exit, or always having a cell phone available. Not surprisingly, most patients with panic disorder have at least mild agoraphobia (White & Barlow, 2002).

What Can You Do?

It is normal for new moms to experience a myriad of physical symptoms associated with panic. The hormonal adjustments after childbirth certainly play a role. Furthermore, many other aspects of being a new mom can lead to uncomfortable panic-like symptoms. Listening to one's baby cry can cause acceleration in heart rate. Sleep deprivation, as well as not eating and drinking enough, can cause dizziness or lightheadedness. New moms can experience the cognitive symptoms associated with panic, such as fear of losing control or going crazy. Again, sleep deprivation and the normal stress of caring for a newborn can cause us to experience symptoms we never experienced before.

Particularly for new moms who never experienced panic symptoms before having a baby, it is important to first see your doctor to rule out any medical problems. Panic attacks can be caused by thyroid abnormalities, which can occur during the postpartum period. Panic symptoms can also be brought on by the use of substances. Many sleep-deprived new moms rely on caffeine to keep them alert. Consider whether your caffeine intake might be accounting for some panic symptoms that you are experiencing. After medical problems or the effects of substances such as caffeine have been ruled out, there are many effective ways to deal with panic attacks and panic disorder.

For moms who are experiencing panic *symptoms* but who do not have panic disorder (meaning that they have the symptoms, but don't fear them or change their behavior based on them), there are simple things to do to prevent the progression into a full-blown disorder. As with intrusive thoughts, it is important not to make too much of these symptoms. It is fine to notice them ("Gee, my heart is racing"), but the key is to not worry about them. Remind yourself that these physical symptoms are not dangerous; they are simply brought on by all the physical changes and stresses associated with being a new mom.

The question of behavior change in response to panic symptoms is a tricky one. You should *not* change your behavior in direct response to a panic symptom. If your heart begins to race, let it race. Don't change your behavior because you are experiencing a panic symptom. If you are feeling light-headed one morning and are tempted to stay home for fear of fainting at the grocery store, head out to the grocery store as soon as possible! When people go about their business *despite feeling anxious,* two important learning experiences occur. First, people learn that panic symptoms go away without special intervention. Second, people learn that panic symptoms are not dangerous. These two insights can make a difference between a short-lived bout of panic symptoms and the evolution of these symptoms into a full-blown panic disorder.

At the same time, it is prudent to take a look at what might be contributing to panic symptoms and be proactive about making behavioral changes that might reduce them. If you are drinking five cups of coffee each day, cut back gradually. If you are on a severely restrictive diet to try to lose that baby weight, now might be a time to increase your caloric intake of healthful, high-energy foods. If you always found exercise or yoga calming, reintegrate these activities into your life. Making healthy lifestyle changes is very different from responding to a harmless panic symptom as it is happening.

For new moms who have a full-blown case of panic disorder with or without agoraphobia, there are many effective and efficient treatments available. Both antidepressants and cognitive behavior therapy have been shown effective in the treatment of panic disorder (see Kase & Roth Ledley, 2007, for a review). CBT for panic disorder involves three main components—cognitive restructuring (challenging beliefs about the danger of physical symptoms), interoceptive exposure (purposefully bringing on the scary physical symptoms in order to learn that they are not dangerous), and in vivo exposure (going into feared and avoided situations to learn that nothing bad is going to happen—even if you feel panicky). The idea of exposure therapy can seem daunting to people who go to great lengths to avoid stimuli that bring on panic symptoms. However, exposures within CBT are done in a systematic way. Prior to doing exposures, patients learn helpful cognitive coping strategies that they did not have before beginning therapy. Exposures are done gradually, beginning with the least-feared situations and working up to the most-feared situations. Furthermore, exposures are often done for the first time in the presence of the therapist. The therapist provides support, helping patients to remain in their feared situations until anxiety decreases and they see that their feared outcomes did not occur.

For mild cases of panic disorder, busy new moms might benefit from reading a self-help book such as *Mastery of Your Anxiety and Panic* (Barlow & Craske, 2006) and working through exposures on their own or with a trusted friend.

OBSESSIVE–COMPULSIVE DISORDER

Obsessive–compulsive disorder is characterized by the presence of obsessions or compulsions. Typically, obsessions and compulsions go hand in hand and are functionally related to one another. Obsessions are defined as "recurrent and persistent thoughts, impulses, or images that are experienced . . . as intrusive and inappropriate and that cause marked anxiety or distress" (American Psychiatric Association, 1994, p. 422). In response to the anxiety caused by obsessions, patients with OCD engage in compulsions or rituals. Rituals are meant to decrease or prevent the experience of anxiety and prevent the occurrence of feared consequences. Rituals can be overt behaviors (such as hand-washing) or mental acts (such as saying a prayer or counting up to a certain number to prevent bad things from happening). As an example, a person with contamination concerns might worry that they will contract an illness after touching a doorknob (obsession). In response to the anxiety brought on by this obsession, this person might pull out their hand sanitizer as soon as possible (compulsion/ritual). Engaging in the ritual is meant to reduce anxiety and prevent feared outcomes (contracting an illness). Certainly, many new moms worry about germs and liberally use hand sanitizer to prevent illness. Clinically significant OCD, however, is associated with significant distress (e.g., becoming extremely anxious after being out in public places or when simply thinking about being around other people) and functional impairment (e.g., taking a very long shower to prevent germ transmission instead of spending time with baby, avoiding going out in public at all to prevent illness).

When lay people think about OCD, they typically associate it with *washing* and *checking*. These are, in fact, common subtypes of OCD. People respond to contamination concerns (e.g., worrying that their baby will contract a deadly illness from exposure to germs) with excessive washing and cleaning rituals (e.g., hand washing, long showers, excessive cleaning of household items). People respond to safety concerns (e.g., worrying that the house will burn down and kill everyone inside) with checking rituals (e.g., checking the stove, candles, etc.). Avoidance is also an important part of OCD. A patient who fears contamination might avoid taking her baby out of the house or might go to great lengths to avoid exposure to germs if they do go out (e.g., Mom might wear gloves, even in warm weather). A patient who fears that her house will burn down might completely avoid lighting candles or turning on the stove.

It is important to recognize that obsessions tend to be slightly more unusual or less reality-based than everyday worries. Although many moms worry about their babies getting colds or stomach bugs, a mom with OCD might worry about her baby developing autism because of exposure to chemical contaminants. I treated a mom with this concern, and her fears were so far-reaching that she avoided pumping gas when her baby was in the car, refused to use household cleaners at home, and would not hold her baby on park benches because the wood might have been treated with chemicals.

Other subtypes of OCD also exist. Some moms might fear acting on unwanted sexual or aggressive impulses. For example, I worked with a mom who feared hurting her baby with a knife as she made dinner or inadvertently putting the baby in the garbage disposal or in the oven. In response to these obsessions, this patient had her husband hide all their knives and scissors, and she completely avoided bringing her baby into the kitchen. Even when her baby was safely in her crib, she checked on her repeatedly to make sure she had not harmed her and "forgotten." She also avoided all news stories about moms who harmed their babies for fear that she would "get an idea." Other presentations of OCD include fear of making mistakes, fear of throwing things away, and fear of sinning or having blasphemous thoughts. These kinds of worries tend to be more frequent and more intense, and have more irrational content, than those experienced by people without OCD.

What Can You Do?

Obsessions tend to be slightly more unusual or less reality-based than everyday worries. This can cause people to worry that they are "going crazy" and might actually act on their thoughts. It is essential to emphasize that people with OCD do not act on their thoughts. Rather, because they find their thoughts totally incongruent with their true desires and feelings, they go to excessive lengths to prevent harm from coming to themselves or others. This was illustrated in the previous paragraphs in the example of the patient who feared harming her baby. She went to excessive lengths to make sure she would not act on obsessions that were so completely incongruent with the love she felt for her baby.

It can be all but impossible for an individual in the throes of OCD to feel confident that he or she is not going crazy or is not on the verge of acting on a terrible thought. It is essential to seek help from a mental health professional who specializes in OCD (check out the Web site for the Obsessive–Compulsive Foundation, http://www.ocfoundation.org, to find a professional in your area). She or he will be able to do a thorough assessment to establish the diagnosis of OCD and to educate you about the disorder. Often, just a few sessions of education about the nature of OCD can greatly reduce the distress experienced by people who suffer from it.

There are two treatment approaches that have been shown to be effective in the research literature—antidepressant medication and a form of CBT called exposure and ritual (or response) prevention (EX/RP). EX/RP involves exposure to situations that bring on obsessions while concurrently resisting the urge to ritualize. Let's return to my patient who feared harming her baby while cooking dinner. Our work involved gradually getting her and her baby into the kitchen to cook dinner. Exposures included turning the garbage disposal on while the baby was in her bouncy seat on the kitchen floor, turning the garbage disposal on while holding the baby, turning the stove on while the baby was in the kitchen, and using knives when the baby was in the kitchen. Throughout these exposures, we kept an eye out for rituals, including checking the baby for burns and cuts after dinnertime. We also read numerous news stories about moms who had harmed their babies while ensuring that my patient did not engage in any mental rituals to decrease her anxiety (e.g., reassuring herself that she would never do such a thing). Doing these exposures concurrent with ritual prevention led to a significant decrease in obsessions and compulsive behaviors and to a significant improvement in this mom's quality of life.

As discussed in the section on panic disorder, the idea of exposure therapy can be frightening to people who have gone out of their way to avoid feared stimuli. However, EX/RP is carried out in a systematic way. Treatment begins with exposure to the patient's least-feared stimuli. Often, by the time patients encounter their most feared situation it does not seem scary anymore because they had so many opportunities to see that feared outcomes did not occur following exposures. Furthermore, trained therapists are skilled at helping patients manage anxiety and stay in an exposure situation long enough to see their anxiety decrease and to learn that feared outcomes are highly unlikely to occur.

Individuals with mild cases of OCD might be able to do exposure and ritual prevention treatment on their own with the help of widely available books such as *Stop Obsessing: How to Overcome Your Obsessions and Compulsions* (Foa & Wilson, 2001) and *Mastery of Obsessive–Compulsive Disorder: A Cognitive–Behavioral Approach, Client Workbook* (Foa & Kozak, 2005). If you have read one of these books and given treatment a try on your own with little success, do seek the help of a mental health professional with expertise in the treatment of OCD. Sometimes even a couple of sessions can help you get started with treatment and allow you to continue on your own.

PUTTING IT ALL TOGETHER

I hope you have learned two important lessons from this appendix. First, mood fluctuations and anxiety are a normal part of new motherhood. Even significant problems such as PPD, OCD, and panic disorder affect many new moms. Fortunately, all these problems are treatable. The tips presented in this appendix should prevent minor mood fluctuations and anxious thoughts from evolving into more significant problems. For new moms whose symptoms are already at a level at which PPD or an anxiety disorder can be diagnosed, guidelines are provided for seeking out professional help. The most important thing to remember is that getting help for these problems is not a sign of weakness. Rather, it is a sign of strength. Not only will getting help benefit you but it will also benefit your new baby. You will have the energy to care for your little one, the strength to deal with the inevitable challenges, and the clarity of mind to enjoy all the pleasures inherent in being a new mom.

RESOURCES FOR NEW MOMS

Every new mom has her favorite resources; these are mine. I want to emphasize that I have no financial ties to any of the companies, authors, organizations, or Web sites listed here, with the exceptions of my own Web site (http://www.thecalmmom.com) and the publisher of *Becoming a Calm Mom*, the American Psychological Association. All the resources listed are those I have found helpful in my role as a new mom and are consistent with the approach taken within *Becoming a Calm Mom*.

WAYS TO CONNECT WITH OTHER NEW MOMS

Participate in Exercise Programs

There are many ways to get exercise with your baby in tow! Beyond the obvious benefits of exercise for you and fresh air for your little one, you will meet other new moms at baby-friendly exercise programs. Check out large national programs such as Baby Boot Camp (http://www.babybootcamp.com) and See Mommy Run (http://www.seemommyrun.com). You can inquire at local gyms and community centers for similar programs in your area.

Join a Moms Club

The International Moms Clubs (http://www.momsclub.org) is a support group for stay-at-home moms. There are more than 2,000 chapters in the United States. Groups meet during the day, and children are welcome.

Do Something You Used to Like to Do Before You Became a Mom and Bring Your Baby Along

Did you know that in many cities you can go to a movie with your baby? Go to your favorite Internet search engine and type *reel moms* and the name of your city to see whether this resource is available where you live. Do you like the arts or learning about the history and culture of your city? Check out Metropolitan Moms (http://www.metropolitanmoms.com), a program that arranges cultural opportunities for new moms, with baby along for the fun. The program is currently only in New York and Philadelphia but is expanding to many other cities. The benefit of activities like these is that you will meet other women who share your interests and who share the experience of being a new mom. If you can't find an organized program in your area to meld your interests with your desire to connect with other moms, start one! Put up signs in your local grocery store and bookstore or post a message in Internet chat rooms or forums frequented by new moms in your area.

Take Your Baby to a Class

There are many fun classes, even for very young babies (one widely available program in the United States and Canada is Gymboree, http://www.gymboreeclasses.com). Check out your community newspaper and magazines for local music classes, gym classes, story times at the public library, and baby or tot programs at churches and synagogues. Your baby will enjoy seeing other little ones, and you will get to meet other moms.

RESOURCES FOR BREAST-FEEDING MOMS

Joining a breast-feeding support group can have two advantages: (a) by receiving support from a facilitator and fellow breast-feeding moms, you are more likely to persevere with breast-feeding, and (b) you will meet lots of other new moms who might be a great source of friendship and support even after you have stopped nursing your baby. To find a local support group or a lactation consultant to meet with one-on-one, contact the La Leche League (1-800-LALECHE or http://www.lalecheleague.org). You can also learn about resources for breast-feeding moms by asking the nurses at the hospital where you gave birth or asking your obstetrician or pediatrician.

BOOKS FOR NEW MOMS THAT ARE CONSISTENT WITH THE CALM MOM APPROACH

For information on establishing good sleep habits for new babies and new moms, consult the following books by pediatric sleep expert Dr. Jodi Mindell.

Mindell, J. (2005). *Sleeping through the night: How infants, toddlers, and their parents can get a good night's sleep* (Rev. ed.). New York: Harper Collins.
Mindell, J. (2007). *Sleep deprived no more: From pregnancy to early motherhood—helping you and your baby sleep through the night.* New York: Marlowe & Company.

For succinct, insightful information on infant and toddler development, turn to the "Dean of American Pediatrics," T. Berry Brazelton. One of the strengths of this book and others by Dr. Brazelton lies in the emphasis on helping parents see baby behavior from the baby's point of view (rather than taking everything so personally!).

Brazelton, T. B. (2006). *Touchpoints: Birth to 3, your child's emotional and behavioral development* (2nd Rev. ed.). New York: Da Capo Press.

Discipline? For babies? Yes, it is never too early to start. This book includes great basic information on infant development and temperament, as well as helpful tips on sleeping and feeding. It also helps new parents see how they can start laying the groundwork for well-behaved children early on in life.

Nelson, J., Erwin, C., & Duffy, R. (1998). *Positive discipline: The first three years, from infant to toddler—laying the foundation for raising a capable, confident child.* New York: Three Rivers Press.

As I discuss in *Becoming a Calm Mom*, even the strongest relationship can take a hit when baby arrives. The best book I have read on how to weather the storm when "baby makes three" is by John and Julie Gottman, internationally recognized researchers on relationships.

Gottman, J. M., & Gottman, J. S. (2007). *And baby makes three: The six-step plan for preserving marital intimacy and rekindling romance after baby arrives.* New York: Crown Publishers.

WEB SITES FOR NEW MOMS

- Baby Center (http://www.babycenter.com). This amazing Web site sends an e-mail each week about what you can expect from your little one's development. Helpful links provide new moms with all sorts of information, from age-appropriate games to play with your baby to helping your baby sleep through the night. The site also contains great information for new moms on postbaby body image, postpartum depression, finding good child care, and pretty much any other topic you can think of!

- American Academy of Pediatrics (http://www.aap.org). There is a lot of information out there on infant health and development. This Web site is unbiased and based on science. The Web site includes a listing of the many wonderful AAP publications (I particularly like *Caring for Your Baby and Young Child: Birth to Age 5* for health-related questions). The Web site also includes a "Find a Pediatrician" function that is particularly useful for parents who need to find a specialist, such as a developmental pediatrician, in their area.

- Working Mother Magazine (http://www.workingmother.com). Great online articles relevant to working moms and excellent opportunities to connect with other working moms.

- The Calm Mom (http://www.thecalmmom.com). This is my Web site, which has much the same spirit as *Becoming a Calm Mom*. The site includes tips for becoming a calmer mom and monthly hot topics of interest to new moms.

RESOURCES FOR MOMS WITH POSTPARTUM DEPRESSION AND ANXIETY

For more information on postpartum depression, see the following.

- http://www.womenshealth.gov/faq/postpartum.htm
- http://www.postpartum.net

For more information on postpartum anxiety:

- http://www.adaa.org/GettingHelp/MFarchives/Monthly Features(January).asp

There are many excellent books on postpartum depression. I strongly recommend the following:

Kleiman, K. R., & Raskin, V. D. (1994). *This isn't what I expected: Overcoming postpartum depression.* New York: Bantam Books.

FINDING A THERAPIST

These Web sites are helpful for finding a therapist in your area:

- American Psychological Association Psychologist Locator (http://locator.apa.org/)
- *Psychology Today,* The Therapy Directory (http://therapists.psychologytoday.com/rms/prof_search.php)
- Association for Behavioral and Cognitive Therapies, Find a Therapist (http://www.abct.org/members/Directory/Find_A_Therapist.cfm) (Note: This is a good resource for therapists who can treat postpartum anxiety and depression. To narrow in further on therapists trained in the treatment of obsessive–compulsive disorder, consult the Web site for the Obsessive–Compulsive Foundation, http://www.ocfoundation.org.)
- Dr. Karen Kleiman's Web site provides excellent advice for seeking help with postpartum depression (http://www.postpartumstress.com/where_can_i_get_help.html)

NOTES

CHAPTER ONE

Hayes, S. C. (2005). *Get out of your mind and into your life: The new acceptance and commitment therapy.* Oakland, CA: New Harbinger Publications.

Rajneesh. (n.d.). Retrieved April 9, 2008, from http://thinkexist.com/quotes/bhagwan_shree_rajneesh/

Quindlen, A. (2003, May 3). [May calendar].

Stanton, E. C. (2002). *Eighty years and more: 1815–1897, Reminiscenses of Elizabeth Cady Stanton.* Lebanon, NH: University Press of New England. (Original work published in 1898)

CHAPTER FOUR

American Academy of Pediatrics. (2004). *Caring for your baby and young child: Birth to age 5.* New York: Bantam Books.

Brazelton, T. B. (2006). *Touchpoints: Birth to 3, your child's emotional and behavioral development* (2nd rev. ed.). New York: Da Capo Press.

Golinkoff, R. M., & Hirsch-Pasek, K. (1999). *How babies talk: The magic and mystery of language in the first three years of life.* New York: Plume.

Li, R., Darling, N., Maurice, E., Barker, L., & Grummer-Strawn, L. M. (2005). Breast-feeding rates in the United States by characteristics of the child, mother, or family: The 2002 National Immunization Survey. *Pediatrics, 115,* 31–37.

Maas, J. (2008). *Tips for parents of newborns, toddlers, and children.* Retrieved April 9, 2008, from http://www.powersleep.org/lifecycle.htm

Mindell, J. (2005). *Sleeping through the night: How infants, toddlers, and their parents can get a good night's sleep* (Rev. ed.). New York: HarperCollins.

CHAPTER FIVE

Ellis, A. (1998). *How to control your anxiety before it controls you.* Secaucus, NJ: Carol Publishing Group.

Winnicott, D. W. (1993). *Talking to parents.* Cambridge, MA: Perseus Publishing.

CHAPTER SIX

American Academy of Pediatrics. (2004). *Caring for your baby and young child: Birth to age 5.* New York: Bantam Books.

National Institute of Child Health and Human Development. (n.d.). *Study of early child care and youth development.* Retrieved May 20, 2008, from http://secc.rti.org/

Ross, C. E., & Mirowsky, J. (1992). Households, employment, and the sense of control. *Social Psychology Quarterly, 55,* 217–235.

Tingey, H., Kiger, G., & Riley, P. J. (1996). Juggling multiple roles: Perceptions of working mothers. *Social Science Journal, 33,* 183–191.

U.S. Census Bureau. (2003). *Fertility of American women June 2002: Population characteristics.* Retrieved May 20, 2008, from http://www.census.gov/prod/2003pubs/p20-548.pdf

CHAPTER SEVEN

Gottman, J. M., & Gottman, J. S. (2007). *And baby makes three: The six-step plan for preserving marital intimacy and rekindling romance after baby arrives.* New York: Crown Publishers.

APPENDIX

Abramowitz, J. S., Schwartz, S. A., & Moore, K. M. (2003). Obsessional thoughts in postpartum females and their partners: Content, severity and relationship with depression. *Journal of Clinical Psychology in Medical Settings, 10,* 157–164.

American Psychiatric Association. (1994). *Diagnostic and statistical manual of mental disorders* (4th ed.). Washington, DC: Author.

Barlow, D. H., & Craske, M. G. (2006). *Mastery of your anxiety and panic: Client workbook* (4th ed.). New York: Oxford University Press.

Beck, A. T., Rush, A. J., Shaw, B., & Emery, G. (1979). *Cognitive therapy of depression.* New York: Guilford Press.

Foa, E. B., & Wilson, R. (2001). *Stop obsessing: How to overcome your obsessions and compulsions* (2nd ed.). New York: Bantam Books.

Foa, E. B., & Kozak, M. J. (2005). *Mastery of obsessive–compulsive disorder: A cognitive–behavioral approach: Client workbook.* New York: Oxford University Press.

Grace, S. L., Evindar, A., & Stewart, D. E. (2003). The effect of postpartum depression on child cognitive development and behavior: A review and critical analysis of the literature. *Archives of Women's Mental Health, 6,* 263–274.

Kase, L., & Roth Ledley, D. (2007). *Anxiety disorders* (Wiley Concise Guides to Mental Health). Hoboken, NJ: Wiley.

Miller, L. J., & Rukstalis, M. (1999). Beyond the "blues": Hypotheses about postpartum reactivity. In L. J. Miller (Ed.), *Postpartum mood disorders* (pp. 3–19). Washington, DC: American Psychiatric Press.

Parents. (2007, November). [Miscellaneous note].

Payne, J. L. (2007). Antidepressant use in the postpartum period: Practical considerations. *American Journal of Psychiatry, 164,* 1329–1332.

White, K. S., & Barlow, D. H. (2002). Panic disorder and agoraphobia. In D. H. Barlow (Ed.), *Anxiety and its disorders: The nature and treatment of anxiety and panic* (2nd ed., pp. 328–379). New York: Guilford Press.

INDEX

ABOUT THE AUTHOR

Deborah Roth Ledley, PhD, is associate director of the Adult Anxiety Clinic of Temple University in Philadelphia, Pennsylvania, and also maintains a private practice in Plymouth Meeting, Pennsylvania. Dr. Ledley has published over 40 articles and book chapters on the nature and treatment of anxiety disorders. She has also published three books: *Wiley Concise Guides to Mental Health: Anxiety Disorders* (2007); *Improving Outcomes and Preventing Relapse in Cognitive–Behavioral Therapy* (2005); and the bestselling *Making Cognitive–Behavioral Therapy Work: Clinical Process for New Practitioners* (2005). Dr. Ledley is the founder of a Web site for new moms called *TheCalmMom.com.* She lives in suburban Philadelphia with her husband and two small children, who inspired her to develop this Web site and to write *Becoming a Calm Mom.*